A LITTLE BOOK OF
RUGBY
UNION

· A LITTLE BOOK OF RUGBY ·

ALLSORTED.

This edition first published in Great Britain in 2024
by Allsorted Ltd, WD19 4BG, U.K.

The facts and statistics in this book are correct up to the end of the 2023/24 season. The data comes from publicly available sources and is presented as correct as far as our knowledge allows. The opinions in this book are personal and individual and are not affiliated to the football club in any way. Any views or opinions represented in this book are personal and belong solely to the book author and do not represent those of people, institutions or organisations that the football club or publisher may or may not be associated with in professional or personal capacity, unless explicitly stated. Any views or opinions are not intended to malign any religious, ethnic group, club, organisation, company or individual.

All rights reserved. No part of this work may be reproduced in any form or by any means, electronic or mechanical, including photocopying, recording or by any information storage and retrieval system, without the prior written permission of the publisher.

© Susanna Geoghegan Gift Publishing
Author: Magnus Allan
Cover design: Milestone Creative
Contents design: Bag of Badgers Ltd
Illustrations: Ludovic Sallé

ISBN: 978-1-915902-61-0

Printed in China

• A LITTLE BOOK OF RUGBY •

★ CONTENTS ★

Introduction	5	Sarah Hunter	66	Gareth Edwards	122
Colin Deans	8	Rugby boots	70	Rugby School & American football	125
Test point-takers	12	Martin Johnson	72	Speak to me like that again ...	126
The whole Webb Ellis thing	15	The break from London	76	The Triple Crown	128
J.P.R. Williams	18	Dan Carter	78	Gary Armstrong	130
Work hard, play hard	20	Bledisloe Cup	80	The Cook Cup/ Ella-Mobbs Trophy	133
Brian O'Driscoll	22	The British & Irish Lions	83	The fart that cracked a mountain	135
Rugby: What took you so long?	26	Most Test tries	86	Jason Robinson	138
Antoine Dupont	28	The Tom Richards Cup	88	Mouthguards	140
Tests played	30	Bryan Habana	90	World Cup points	142
The catalyst for rugby's explosive growth	32	Free for all and all for one	94	Accovacciarsi ...	144
Sam Warburton	34	Gavin Hastings	98	Rugby and the Olympics	147
From playing fields to Pall Mall	36	The Calcutta Cup	100	Centenary Quaich trophy	149
The Gould affair	38	George Gregan	102	Who goes where?	151
Lawrence Dallaglio	42	The Barbarians	106	Jonny Wilkinson	154
Rugby belongs to Italy?	46	Gaelic football	108	The man in seat 64J	158
The ball	49	Jonah Lomu	110		
Most capped Test players	56	Why sing the National Anthem?	113		
Why 'try'?	59	Gil Evans' whistle	116		
Women's rugby	62	The Freethy florin	119		
		Rugby School & Aussie rules	120		

· A LITTLE BOOK OF RUGBY ·

"I love what rugby is: brains as well as brawn and then beer afterwards."

Scottish scrum-half Roy Laidlaw has a simple opinion of rugby's three-B appeal.

★ INTRODUCTION ★

Rugby union's a messy old business. It's a sport that's built for the mud of winter because the ground's too hard to fall on at any other time of year.

Two teams of 15 players spending 80 minutes chasing a ball around a field is always going to make a bit of churn. But when some of those players are mobile walls of solid human and they are trying to steamroller their way through an opposition's equally mobile walls of solid human as two groups of agile and only fractionally less solid slabs of human try to dance around and through them all, it's not a massive surprise that things can get messy. It's a good job that grass grows quickly.

To the untrained eye, the action on the pitch can seem bewildering, but there's a well-defined choreography and a great deal of tactical subtlety underneath the shouting and the crunching tackles.

Rugby's commitment to its amateur status caused a lot of tensions and rifts throughout its first century or so, but the decision to become professional in 1995 marked a very clear turning point for the game. Professionalism raised expectations and commitment at the top of the game and means that the modern era is more highly represented in the legends of the sport simply because if you are training to play rugby day in, day out, you are likely to be better at the sport than if you are working as a lawyer or a miner during the day and dabbling in a bit of rugby at the weekend. It's also why the stats for the most-capped players are completely dominated by players from the modern era.

Everyone's right to exist

The thing about rugby is that despite what people from the south of England, over the wall in Scotland or down in the valleys of Wales might have you believe, there are, in fact, several different versions of the game. Probably the most prominent of these, in Britain at least, is rugby league, an offshoot formed at the end of the 19th century when a drove of northerners got snotty about a gaggle of southerners being snooty (see page 76), stormed up to the George Hotel in Huddersfield and formed a breakaway structure. The rebels might have already been kicked out of the union first in a yah-boo-sucks kind of way, but that depends on who you ask.

The point is that this is a book predominantly focused on what has subsequently become known as 'rugby union'. There are other forms of rugby football out there and nobody wants to disrespect them, deny their valid view of history or right to exist (purely through self-preservation, given the size of many of the players these days), but for simplicity's sake, when this book talks about rugby, it's talking about rugby union unless otherwise stated.

Complicating matters is the whole football aspect. Rugby union is technically also known as 'rugby football', because back in the day, all sports that were played by teams chasing a ball in some way or other were known as 'football', whether hands were involved or not. The version of football played at Rugby School evolved into rugby football, and then rugby union (following the schism that resulted in the formation of rugby league). This is why Aussie rules football, which was developed by a former Rugby School pupil (see page 120), is actually a form of rugby rather than a form of what we know today as football.

Similarly, this book will refer to the town of Rugby as 'Rugby town' where applicable. It turns out that it is possible to have too much rugby, even in a book about rugby.

Clear? Good. Let's move on.

· A LITTLE BOOK OF RUGBY ·

★ COLIN DEANS ★
(SCOTLAND)

The Scottish borders have a long and storied history with rugby, with plenty of legendary players emerging from Reiver territory. Colin Deans was raised on a string of tales about Hawick's famous rugby players and dreamed of pulling on the town's famous green jersey. At the age of nine, he was taught by Bill McLaren, a primary school teacher who happened to be the voice of rugby union commentary in his spare time from 1953 until 2002. McLaren helped spot Deans' talent, marked him out as a potentially useful hooker and encouraged him to make his way through the ranks. Deans became a key part of the Scottish team between 1978 and 1987.

Deans should have played for the British and Irish Lions, but was an unused sub in 1983, kept on the bench by the Lions captain who happened to be a fellow hooker. Three years later, he was undoubtedly the best hooker in Britain or Ireland but the tour was cancelled due to the political situation in South Africa. He had the consolation of leading the Lions in a match against a Rest of the World XV on a blustery night in Cardiff, but it was small solace.

On a brighter note, Deans was part of the 1984 team that delivered Scotland its first Five Nations Grand Slam since 1925, with his mobility, speed and exceptional line-outs proving to be decisive.

He was capped 52 times in total for Scotland, skippering the team when they mauled England 33–6 in 1986 and making sure that the bar bill for the celebration found its way on to the England captain's room number. It's amazing what they could do in the days before professionalism.

Deans was on the pitch for one Scotland's most famous victories. In 1983, Scotland took England 22-12 – at Twickenham no less; a feat that would not be achieved for another 38 years, but sometimes what the spectators see is different from what's actually going on down on the pitch.

For the watching Scots, the victory was legendary; for the English, humbling, but Deans later described the day as simply horrendous. He'd been sharing a room with Ian Milne, a prop who was most of the time known as The Bear (due more to his size and strength than what he might or might not have got up to in the woods.) Unfortunately, this wasn't most of the time. Milne had picked up a stomach bug and had been up half the night and by the time of the England match, Deans was starting to feel pretty ropey himself.

He fought through the nausea but was allegedly gladder than most other people to hear the final whistle so he could get off the pitch.

'Rugby for me is family. I think of the guys all the time.'

Colin Deans, legend and decent bloke.

Player	Country
Andrew Mehrtens	(New Zealand, 1995–2004)
Stephen Jones	(Wales/British & Irish Lions, 1998–2011)
Diego Domínguez	(Argentina/Italy, 1989-2003)
Florin Vlaicu	(Romania, 2006–2022)
Ronan O'Gara	(Ireland/British & Irish Lions, 2000–2013)
Neil Jenkins	(Wales/British & Irish Lions, 1990–2003)
Johnny Sexton	(Ireland/British & Irish Lions, 2009–2023)
Jonny Wilkinson	(England/British & Irish Lions, 1998–2011)
Owen Farrell	(England/British & Irish Lions, 2012–present)
Dan Carte	(New Zealand, 2003–2015)

★ TEST POINT-TAKERS ★

·A LITTLE BOOK OF RUGBY·

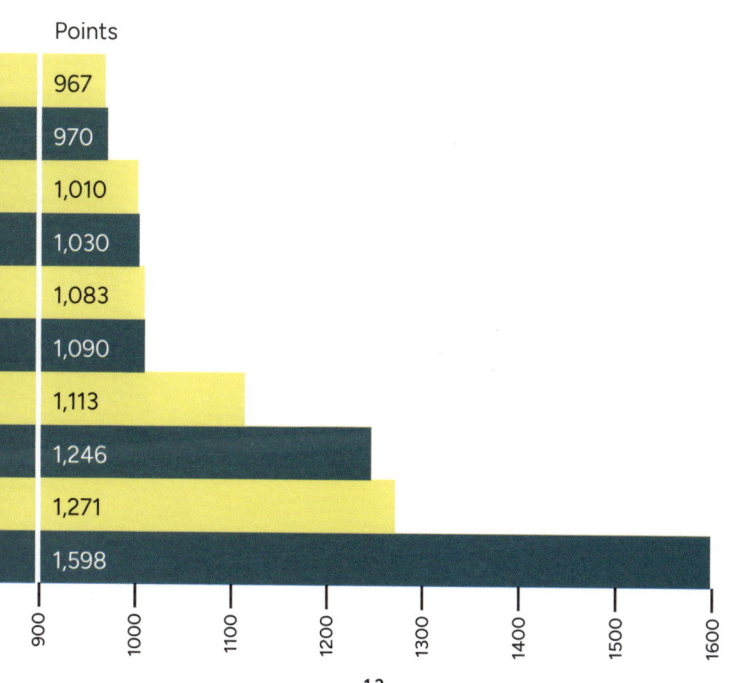

• A LITTLE BOOK OF RUGBY •

"I've seen a lot of people like him, but they weren't playing on the wing."

All Blacks icon Colin Meads reflects on the majesty of Jonah Lomu.

★ THE WHOLE WEBB ELLIS THING ★

On 10 May 1823, William Webb Ellis, a pupil at Rugby School, one of the oldest fee-paying schools in England, is said to have picked up the ball in the middle of a game of football and run with it towards the goal line. His classmates chased him, and a new sport was born. Allegedly.

The problem with the story is that the first time it was ever mentioned in print was more than half a century later in 1876 in a letter to the Rugby School newspaper (yes, that posh) written by a former pupil who had heard about it from a friend of a friend.

So, that's not to say that it's not true; it's probably just worth taking with a pinch of salt.

The bottom line is that back in those days, pupils at Rugby School (and many of the other private schools up and down the land) tended to set up and manage their own games without the involvement of the teachers. This meant that the rules of the games they played evolved each year according to the players' whims.

So, it's possible that Webb Ellis picked up the ball and ran with it because he was struck by inspiration to create a whole new game of football. It's equally possible that he was having a tantrum about something, went to take his ball away and was chased down and jumped on by his classmates who then decided that it was all jolly good fun and they should do it again tomorrow just to teach Webb Ellis a lesson for being such a terrible prig.

He may even have been in the science block at the time, obliviously checking the results of an experiment with pigs' bladders and simply got his name added to the incident 50 years later because no one could remember that it was actually little James Thornton-Willington-Smythe who picked up the ball and ran with it.

The Webb Ellis thing is a nice story – it might have some elements of truth to it – and it's a nice name to stick on a cup but, in the end, we'll never know the true story. At the same time, it might not really matter.

"The main difference between league and union is that now I get my hangovers on Monday instead of Sunday,"

reflected Wales and Lions player Tommy David, who switched codes late in his career.

• A LITTLE BOOK OF RUGBY •

★ J.P.R. WILLIAMS ★
(WALES)

J.P.R. Williams was known as John for the first four years of his career, morphing into J.P.R. (his initials are John Peter Rhys) after a second John (J.J.) Williams emerged onto the scene. The 1970s was a hirsute era, and J.P.R.'s sideburns fitted right in with the fashions, flowing behind him as he surged up from the back. He certainly helped make Five Nations Grand Slams fashionable in Wales in the 1970s, winning in 1971, 1976 and 1978, as well as being a member of six Triple Crown winning teams in 1969, 1971, 1976, 1977, 1978 and 1979.

Williams played for Wales 55 times in total, as well as turning out eight times for the British & Irish Lions over two tours in 1971 and 1974, in New Zealand and South Africa respectively. He would have been part of the 1977 Lions tour as well, but was advised to concentrate on his career as an orthopaedic surgeon.

He played out the back and could fix your back.

Williams was clearly a very talented fellow. Alongside his nascent career as a rugby player, he also won the 1966 British Junior tennis title at Wimbledon, beating David Lloyd 6-4, 6-4. It's not true for everyone, but sometimes with sport, if you've got it, you've really got it.

★ WORK HARD, PLAY HARD ★

For the conspiracy theorists out there, there may be a reason why the legend of Webb Ellis began to emerge after half a century of obscurity.

By the late 1870s, the sport of rugby was starting to approach a fork in the road. Players in the south of England tended to be of the upper and middle classes. They had time to muck about at sport for fun and, frankly, thought that if you were being paid for the experience you were missing out on the gentlemanly spirit of the whole bally adventure, tally-ho, pip-pip. It's supposed to be fun, a chance to blow off steam and teach children the laudable values of hard work, fair play, leadership and camaraderie.

In the working-class north, though, people worked six days a week and if they missed a shift they didn't get paid — so they couldn't afford to be injured, by 'eck. Equally, rugby was starting to become a source of civic pride: large crowds were showing up to see players turn out for their towns' teams. Rugby was fun, it was a chance to release pent-up energy and so on, but it was also a serious business.

Basically, there were two philosophies, both valid, but in utter opposition to each other.

In the midst of all this, there is a hint that the southern rugby authorities needed a story to stamp their ownership on the game. There's a chance that Webb Ellis fitted the bill nicely. Good chap, private school, admittedly from the Midlands, but it could be worse. This was long before the days of public relations consultants, but the Webb Ellis/Rugby School story legitimised the upper class's ownership of the sport and gave them a decent claim to keep dictating how they thought it should be played.

It almost worked.

• A LITTLE BOOK OF RUGBY •

★ BRIAN O'DRISCOLL ★
(IRELAND)

Brian O'Driscoll got over the try line 47 times during his 133 Test matches for his national team, 83 of them as captain. He was the Six Nations Player of the Tournament three times – in 2006, 2007 and 2009 – the highest try scorer in Irish rugby history and the eighth-highest Test try scorer in rugby history. Basically, a decent player to have around.

Having risen through the ranks of the Irish youth system, O'Driscoll gained his first full cap in 1999 during a tour to Australia. His hat trick of tries against France during the 2000 Six Nations helped Ireland win in Paris in the tournament for the first time since 1972. He pulled on the captain's armband for the first time two years later, taking it on a permanent basis in 2003 and leading them to Triple Crowns in 2004, 2006 and 2007. These achievements were topped in 2009 when Ireland won their first Grand Slam in over six decades.

Very few people get the perfect end to an international career: O'Driscoll might just have achieved it. In his final match for Ireland in 2014, his team beat France in Paris for only the second time in four decades and only the third time in six decades. The victory meant that Ireland won the Six Nations. Anything less than a victory would have seen England raise the Cup. O'Driscoll was named man of the match for the second consecutive week (he'd set up two sumptuous tries the week before, during his final home match against Italy). It was the second time he had been on an Ireland team that had won the Championship and only the second time that Ireland had won it since 1985. And that is how you end a career with a flourish.

O'Driscoll stuck with Leinster for his entire career, pulling on the jersey 186 times between 1999 and 2014. They won the Celtic League four times in 2001/02, 2007/08, 2012/13 and 2013/14, with the 2013/14 victory marking O'Driscoll's retirement from club rugby (in the same year as he finished his international career). The victory saw Leinster become the first team to retain the Celtic League title. He also won the European Cup three times in 2008/09, 2010/11 and 2011/12 and the European Challenge Cup in 2012/13.

O'Driscoll's family is steeped in rugby, with his father and his father's cousins playing at the very highest levels.

• A LITTLE BOOK OF RUGBY •

"Knowledge is knowing that a tomato is a fruit, wisdom is knowing not to put it in a fruit salad."

Quite what Brian O'Driscoll did when faced with the tree of knowledge is anyone's guess.

RUGBY: WHAT TOOK YOU SO LONG?

Cricket started to be formalised in around the 1760s, and by the 1780s it was spreading north and west from the south-east of England. Meanwhile, football — in other words, all games played with a foot and a ball, including what we now know as both rugby and football — continued to be fairly unstructured, localised games for the best part of a century. Most of the fee-paying independent schools had their own versions of football (some still do), and it wasn't really until the 1840s that rugby started to spread out of Rugby town and become rugby football.

This begs the question: If cricket was attracting large crowds and people were starting to create clubs by the late 18th and early 19th centuries, why did it take another six decades or so to formalise rugby?

The chances are that it comes down to a simple question of weather and logistics. Roads were very difficult to travel in the winter in the 18th and early 19th centuries in rainy England, so schools and clubs that happily got together to play each other at cricket in the summer struggled to meet up through the mud of winter. By the 1840s, roads were improving and railways were becoming a thing, so it was starting to become easier to get around, even in the depths of winter.

Teams meeting up to play each other created more demand for a uniform set of rules so that they could get on with the business of playing each other rather than quibbling over the rules before kick-off, which is particularly important in a world before floodlights where folk had to get a match played before dusk during the shorter months of the year.

· A LITTLE BOOK OF RUGBY ·

★ ANTOINE DUPONT ★
(FRANCE)

French captain and scrum-half Antoine Dupont started his professional career at Castres before moving over to Toulouse in 2017, going on to win the Top 14, the highest French league, in 2018/19. He then went on to captain the side that won the European Rugby Champions Cup in 2020/21, completing the French rugby double by winning the Top 14 again that season. His Toulouse team went on to impressively repeat the feat in 2023 and 2024.

Having excelled with his 11 international appearances for the French Under-20s side, Dupont joined the senior French team in 2017 and quickly became one of the first names on the team sheet. In 2022, he led the team to a Six Nations Grand Slam.

Dupont was named the Six Nation's best player in 2020, 2022 and 2023, one of only two players, alongside Brian O'Driscoll, to have won the award three times (see page 22). However, he sat out the 2024 tournament so that he could focus on playing for the French Rugby Sevens side for the Olympics in France. Basically, he fancied adding a gold medal to his collection of silverware.

Team	Matches
Argentina (50%)	494
South Africa (63%)	542
Italy (36%)	552
New Zealand (77%)	637
Australia (50%)	684
Scotland (44%)	747
Ireland (48%)	751
Wales (51%)	791
England (56%)	794
France (55%)	817

· A LITTLE BOOK OF RUGBY ·

★ TESTS PLAYED ★

(PERCENTAGE WON IN BRACKETS)

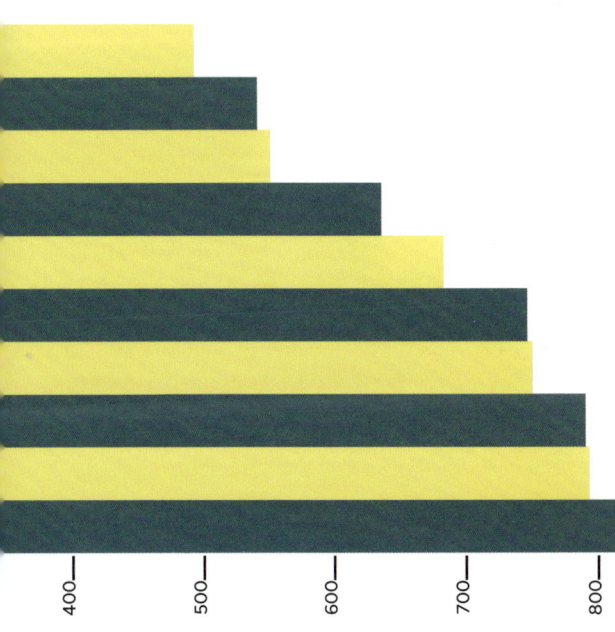

★ THE CATALYST FOR RUGBY'S ★ EXPLOSIVE GROWTH

So why is it that the game of rugby took off? Why don't we spend our Sunday mornings in the autumn and winter playing the Eton field game or Harrow football, both of which exist and arguably come from better-known public schools that could have given them the leg up to become national/international sports?

Basically, it comes down to a book that really sold the whole idea of rugby to the public. *Tom Brown's School Days* was released in 1857 and was a publishing sensation. It was set in the 1830s, was written by someone who had been at Rugby School in the 1830s and 1840s and spent a number of its pages discussing rugby and its importance to the physical, moral and spiritual wellbeing of the boys who played. (It was an all-boys school, don't write in.)

If you think it's a stretch to suggest that a mere book propelled rugby into a global sport, it's worth remembering that there is a Harry Potter-inspired Quidditch league out there today (although it's been rebranded as Quadball – and all broomsticks are kept firmly on the ground), which apparently has more than 600 teams playing in 40 countries. This means that people are still being inspired by games they read about in books.

While we are on the subject of The Boy Who Lived, it's often suggested that *Tom Brown's School Days* provided some of the template for the Harry Potter books. Both feature a child finding their way around an imposing, ancient school with arcane rules and devote pages of their story to sports. If this is the case, this means that Rugby School inspired rugby football, Aussie rules (see page 120) and Quidditch (now Quadball), not to mention the bestselling book series of the 21st century, which isn't bad for a school in a small town in Warwickshire whose only other claims to fame are an imposing cement works and the actor who played the undercover British officer from the TV comedy *'Allo 'Allo* who spoke with the terrible French accent. Apologies if you weren't around during the early 1990s and that reference has gone whizzing over your head.

Meanwhile, Harrow football actually sounds like quite an upmarket name for a sport, but the game is apparently played with a ball that's shaped like an enormous pork pie and includes a form of tackle known as the 'bosh', which … well, if they're happy …

· A LITTLE BOOK OF RUGBY ·

★ SAM WARBURTON ★
(WALES)

Sam Warburton burst onto the international rugby scene in 2009, having captained the Under-18s, Under-19s and Under-20s. So, perhaps saying that he burst onto the scene is a little strong: if you knew anything about rugby, you knew he was coming.

Either way, he made his senior debut against the USA in 2009 and was named as part of the Six Nations squad for 2010. By 2011, he was captaining the national squad regularly, romping through the group stages of the 2011 World Cup and being named best player in Wales' group. He helped take the team to the semi-finals that year.

In 2013, he became the youngest-ever captain of a British & Irish Lions team, heading the tour to Australia and becoming the first Welsh captain of the team since Phil Bennett in 1977. Warburton was captain again for the 2017 tour of New Zealand.

His Cardiff Blues team won the European Challenge Cup in 2009/10 and Wales won the Six Nations in 2012 (with both the Triple Crown and the Grand Slam) and 2013. In total, he represented his country 74 times.

Warburton was in the same class as footballer Gareth Bale at school. The level of competition at school sports days must have been really quite something.

FROM PLAYING FIELDS TO PALL MALL

In the 1850s and early 1860s, football as a whole started to formalise itself. Initially, the two sports that would eventually transmogrify into rugby football and association football were being developed by a group of men operating as the Football Association (FA). By 1863, they had basically come up with a code and a set of rules that most of them could agree to play by.

Some clubs wanted to play the sport slightly differently, though, and there was a lot of focus on two specific aspects of the emerging game. Firstly, they wanted players to be able to catch the ball and run with it in specific circumstances. Secondly, they proposed that if a player was holding the ball, the opposition was entitled to charge, hold, trip or hack at the player (although you weren't allowed to hold and hack a player simultaneously – that would be madness).

The FA's fifth official meeting was the moment when the one sport became two. There was an acrimonious discussion about the decision to remove handling and hacking from the rules of football. The Blackheath Club, which wanted to retain the more physical aspects of the sport, withdrew its support from the FA at its sixth meeting in December 1863, and started to draw together similarly minded clubs that wanted to be able to run with the ball and were a little happier to stick the boot in (in a sporting way).

Eight years later, in January 1871, representatives of 21 clubs from across the south-east of England that were playing versions of rugby got together at the Pall Mall Restaurant in London and started the process of creating the Rugby Football Union (RFU). By coincidence, Pall Mall is named after a game that might have had an influence on the game of golf, but that's another book for another time.

It would allegedly have been 22 clubs if the representative of Wasps hadn't gone to the wrong place on the wrong day at the wrong time. It would have been 23 clubs if the representative of Ealing Rugby Club hadn't stopped for a cheeky half at a different pub on the way and ended up missing the meeting. The uncharitable might suggest that this is why rugby retained its unprofessional status until 1995.

★ THE GOULD AFFAIR ★

Arthur 'Monkey' Gould, so named because he loved climbing trees, was Welsh Rugby's first superstar. Born in 1864, he was one of six brothers, all of whom played for Newport. Three represented Wales at rugby and a fourth found fame on the track as a hurdler in the 1908 Olympics. So, all in all, a family of decent sportspeople.

Gould himself burst onto the scene for Newport at 18, was part of the team's invincible season in 1891/92, scored 37 tries in 24 games of the 1893/94 season and wasn't dropped from the squad until he retired in 1898. He was also on the first Welsh team to beat England and led Wales to their first Triple Crown in 1893. Basically, then, Gould was a handy rugby player who richly deserves the little blue plaque that is displayed on his former home.

That home, though, is the reason why this section is about an incident that rocked rugby to its roots rather than a profile of a rugby player who deserves to be remembered.

Gould was seen as rugby's equivalent of W.G. Grace, the archetypal English Victorian cricketer who popularised that game in the mid- to late-19th century. Cricket held a testimonial match for Grace, and when that was a massive success, someone suggested in 1896 that something similar be held for Gould.

This appeared to be an exceptional idea and turned out to be very popular. A decent chunk of change was donated by people all over Wales, which led to the issue ...

Because what Wales saw as thanking a player for their contribution to the sport, England, Ireland and Scotland saw as blatant professionalism. And professional was the last thing that anyone wanted rugby to be.

To be fair, at the time the sport in England was still smarting from the decision of the northern clubs to break away from the union (see page 76) and Scotland had only recently resolved a long debate about professionalism in soccer and was a little sensitive about the whole money thing (many of their best football players had been heading south of the border where they could be paid for their time and troubles). Also to be fair, the rulebook didn't leave a lot of wiggle room when it stated that players were not permitted to receive money from their club, or from any member of their club, for services rendered to football.

The situation became a stand-off, with Scotland and Ireland refusing to play Wales in the Home Nations Championship in 1897 (England had already played so ended up taking that year's title purely as a result of playing more games. Oh, whoops!). Wales didn't play internationally for another two years.

The Gould affair was resolved with a nod and a wink when the Welsh rugby authorities bought a house for Gould rather than give him money. Gould was banned from playing internationally (he was 34 by this point, so his shoulders would have shrugged if they had anything left in them and his knees probably said thank you), but Wales rejoined the wider rugby community and everyone carried on as they had done before. The rulebook, as you would expect, was quietly tightened up.

Gould continued to be involved in rugby as a referee and an international selector. England and the rest of the home nations continued to stand strong against professionalism wherever there was a risk of it breaking out.

• A LITTLE BOOK OF RUGBY •

"Ballroom dancing is a contact sport. Rugby is a collision sport."

Former South Africa coach Heyneke Meyer pulls no punches.

· A LITTLE BOOK OF RUGBY ·

★ LAWRENCE DALLAGLIO ★
(ENGLAND)

Lorenzo Bruno Nero Dallaglio was an English choirboy who sang backing vocals on Tina Turner's power-ballad *We Don't Need Another Hero (Thunderdome)*, part of the soundtrack for 1980s classic *Mad Max Beyond the Thunderdome*. He also sang at one of the weddings of composer and former occasional member of the House of Lords The Lord Lloyd Webber. He was also a key member of England's victorious 2003 Rugby World Cup squad, although by that time he was going by Lawrence rather than Lorenzo.

Dallaglio played in every minute of the 2003 World Cup campaign, which capped a phenomenal few years as a player and saw him lift the Six Nations Trophy in 1996, 2000, 2001 and 2003 (with a Grand Slam) and the Triple Crown in 1996, 1997, 1998, 2002 and 2003. All in, he was capped 85 times for England, scoring 85 points in the process.

As a Wasps player, he won the Premiership five times, the Powergen Cup three times, the Heineken Cup twice and the Parker Pen Challenge Cup once. The Parker Pen Challenge has subsequently evolved into the EPCR Challenge Cup, rather than being a test that choirboys have to go through if they want to move from writing with a pencil to a big-boy pen. He was also selected for the British & Irish Lions tours of South Africa (1997),

Australia (2001) and New Zealand (2005), although injuries meant he was only capped three times.

All in, a storied career and a valuable addition to any team he played with. Particularly when it came to singing the anthems.

He was never likely to take retirement lying down, so it was no surprise that in 2010 Dallalgio decided to make a charity cycle ride between the Six Nations stadiums – a mere 28,000 km – starting out in Rome and enduring progressively worse weather until he ended up at Murrayfield four weeks later. He has subsequently put himself and his friends through similar challenges every couple of years since, earning significant money for charity and presumably colossal saddle sores along the way.

• A LITTLE BOOK OF RUGBY •

"They were outstanding. They are the best team in the world – by one minute."

Eddie Jones, who coached Australia to second place in the 2003 Rugby World Cup, assesses the winning team's performance.

★ RUGBY BELONGS TO ITALY? ★

While the Webb Ellis story might or might not be true, there are plenty of other games that are held up as potentially influencing the game's development. One strong contender is the Italian 'calcio storico fiorentino' (literally meaning historical kickball from Florence), a game played in Florence since around the 15th century.

It's a brutal game, although the brutality has been toned down a bit in recent years since health and safety went mad and they banned sucker punches, kicks to the head and the release of angry bulls into the playing area. It is reminiscent of rugby in that the forwards go out, try to pin down as many opposition players as possible and then the backs come though with the ball and try to run to a goal line that spans the width of the pitch without getting a hair out of place.

Could it be that an early 19th-century pupil at Rugby School stopped in Florence during a summer tour of Italy, saw the game being played in one of the piazzas and took the idea back to sunny Warwickshire?

Unfortunately, the timelines don't quite fit. The popularity of calcio storico fiorentino is said to have died down in the early 17th century. (Was it the kicks to the head? The goring by bulls?) As a result, it wasn't really being played at the time rugby was being developed; its revival began in the 1920s.

The bottom line is that while games tend to influence each other around the world, if you are going to move a ball across a large pitch, you either have to use your feet, your hands or both. After that, it's just a question of what the aim of the game is: is there a specific goal, an extended scoring area that runs the width of the pitch, or some combination of the two. Rugby has evolved in the way that it has because of gameplay choices that were probably made back in the 1820s and has been finessed in the two centuries since. There are undoubtedly influences from elsewhere, but in the case of calcio storico fiorentino, parallel evolution is more likely than direct descent.

• A LITTLE BOOK OF RUGBY •

"Grandmother or tails, sir?"

A rugby referee to Princess Anne's son Peter Phillips, Gordonstoun School's rugby captain, for his pre-match coin-toss preference.

★ THE BALL ★

The rugby ball has been through something of an evolution over the years. It all started back in 1823 when one Mr William Gilbert, a purveyor of boots and shoes in Rugby town, started to provide balls for nearby Rugby School. He is also said to have sold catapults to pupils ... different times.

Gilbert's balls were four-panelled, hand-stitched affairs made of a pig's bladder encased in leather. Pigs' bladders had three main drawbacks, though. Firstly, pigs come in a variety of shapes and sizes; as a result, Gilbert's balls – although of the highest quality that could be achieved with the technology of the time – were a long way from being a uniform shape and size. This meant that it was difficult to make precise passes or predict where a kick would end up.

The second issue with using pigs' bladders was that if the pig was diseased, it was possible for the person inflating the ball to catch the disease, which in some cases led to death. Which is not the ideal outcome in anyone's career.

The final issue was that the pigs, in the main, quite liked having their bladders where they were, thank you very much.

Health and safety gone mad

Vulcanised rubber started to emerge in the 1860s, just as the sport of rugby was starting to get its act together and create a standardised set of rules (see page 36). By 1862 another of the town of Rugby's rugby ball manufacturers, a chap called Richard Lindon, developed a way to create a more consistent ball using vulcanised rubber — as well as a contraption for inflating it.

Lindon had been spurred into looking beyond pigs' bladders for the rugby ball after he'd lost his wife. She had previously done his inflating, and had died as a result of a pig-related lung infection a few years previously, leaving him to raise their 17 children.

Lindon's inventions made a massive leap forward in consistency for rugby balls, but he didn't patent them — possibly because he was distracted by trying to raise 17 children — so, within a few years, several companies had sprung up using similar processes. This is why the name Gilbert is still associated with the game while Lindon has faded into obscurity. That and the grim story about his wife.

What shape is a rugby ball?

Right, now pay attention class. Today, we are going to be studying the correct name of the shape of the rugby ball. Finney, put Cotton down, he doesn't need that sort of help, thank you very much.

With some sports, it's relatively simple. A ball is a spherical shape, which means that it bounces consistently and most players can judge where it's going to go when it is kicked.

Rugby isn't most sports, though. Rugby has evolved into a game where the ball is often carried and the random bounce adds a satisfying element of chance to a kick, even for the best players.

The rugby ball is known as being egg-shaped, an oval or simply odd. All of these names are incorrect. Evison, I saw you whispering to Berkley, is something amusing you about odd balls? See me after class.

An elongated ellipsoidal ball – a prolate spheroid, in fact! – is used for the game of rugby.

Plumbing the depths, soaring to new heights

Both rugby and football balls started out as an irregular plum shape, but they took separate evolutionary paths, with the rugby ball gradually taking on an elongated ellipsoidal shape. There were three reasons for this.

1. Elongated balls fly better when thrown because an oval shape is more aerodynamic and will move through the air more quickly.

2. Elongated balls are easier to tuck under the arm and run with, but the roundness of the ends also affects the game – the more pointed the ends, the easier it is to pass the ball, but the trickier it is to kick accurately. Rounder ends are easier to control but make passing slower ...

3. It's easier to get some lift under an elongated ball when it's kicked so that it can get over the crossbar to score a goal.

Most importantly, though, the shape of the rugby ball means that no one could mix up a game of rugby with a game of football, which was starting to become an important distinction in the mid- to late-19th century.

It's not rugby that's odd

The only slight issue with this relatively simple tale of evolution in the mid- to late-19th century is that in *Tom Brown's School Days* (published in 1857 about the school in the 1830s – see page 32), a character says at one point that a rugby ball "lies there, quite by itself, in the middle, pointing towards the school goal." This suggests that at least some rugby balls had at least one relatively pointy end even in the early days of the sport.

It's something of a mystery that is unlikely ever to be cleared up. Perhaps some pigs have pointier bladders than others.

It's interesting to note, though, that of all the ball games derived from historical mob football, only soccer and Gaelic football actually use a spherical ball. Both codes of rugby, Aussie rules and Gridiron all use non-spherical balls, so technically it's football that's played with an odd-shaped ball, not rugby.

Leather in the rain

While Lindon's innovations made it possible to bring a more consistent shape to the ball, the leather casing also presented a challenge. The British Isles are huddled between the North Sea and the Atlantic Ocean. Being caught between two large bodies of water means that it rains a lot in the winter and playing fields tend to be muddy between November and March, when the majority of rugby is played. Leather absorbs water, which means that a leather ball of any shape can become heavier and heavier as a game progresses.

Modern synthetic materials offered the solution, and leather was gradually phased out as the 20th century wound to its conclusion, giving us the gloriously consistent, inconsistent rugby ball that we enjoy today.

The size of the ball wasn't actually standardised until 1892, but it's stayed fairly consistent since then, currently coming in at 28–30 cm long, 74–77 cm in circumference (end to end), 58–62 cm maximum width circumference, and weighing between 410 and 460 g. This is slightly smaller than the 1892 version, mostly so it's easier to catch, move and move with.

· A LITTLE BOOK OF RUGBY ·

"What always attracted me was the thrill — some would say the sheer brown-trouser terror — of running out knowing nothing about your opponents. Humiliation or glory, pain or ecstasy, lie ahead. But which will it be?"

Spike Milligan's school days clearly didn't teach him the value of homework when it came to rugby.

Team	Years active
Johnny Sexton (Ireland/British & Irish Lions)	2009–2023
George North (Wales/British & Irish Lions)	2010–2024
Conor Murray (Ireland/British & Irish Lions)	2011–present
Bryan Habana (South Africa)	2004–2016
Rory Best (Ireland)	2005–2019
Aaron Smith (New Zealand)	2012–2023
Michael Hooper (Australia)	2012–2023
Kieran Read (New Zealand)	2008–2019
Victor Matfield (South Africa)	2001–2015
Ben Youngs (England/British & Irish Lions)	2010–2023
Florin Vlaicu (Romania)	2006–2022
Stephen Moore (Australia)	2005–2017
Cian Healy (Ireland)	2009–present
Ronan O'Gara (Ireland/British & Irish Lions)	2000–2013
Keven Mealamu (New Zealand)	2002–2015
James Slipper (Australia)	2010–present
Gethin Jenkins (Wales/British & Irish Lions)	2002–2018
George Gregan (Australia)	1994–2007
Brian O'Driscoll (Ireland/British & Irish Lions)	1999–2014
Sergio Parisse (Italy)	2002–2019
Richie McCaw (New Zealand)	2001–2015
Whitelock (New Zealand)	2010–2023
Alun Wyn Jones (Wales/British & Irish Lions)	2006–2023

★ MOST CAPPED TEST PLAYERS ★

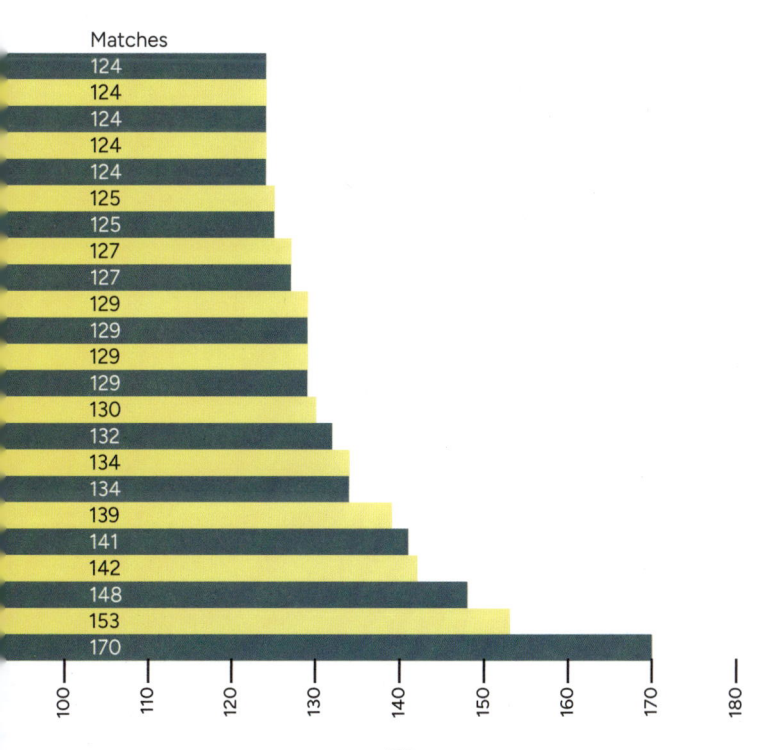

Matches

Matches
124
124
124
124
124
125
125
127
127
129
129
129
129
130
132
134
134
139
141
142
148
153
170

"Rugby is a wonderful show: dance, opera and, suddenly, the blood of a killing."

Richard Burton explains the enduring appeal of rugby, while impressively making everyone feel slightly icky in the process.

Burton's sometimes wife Elizabeth Taylor also had a stated love for rugby, although she drew the line at ear biting.

WHY 'TRY'?

These days, being awarded a try is the primary objective of a game of rugby – but why is it called a 'try'? This being rugby, the answer is simultaneously quite simple and gloriously convoluted.

In the early days of the sport, the winner of a rugby match was simply the team that scored the most goals – in other words, over the crossbar and between the posts. A try simply gave the team that got over the line the chance to have a kick at goal and literally try to score some points. The only time that tries directly counted was if both teams had an equal number of goals, in which case, the team with the most tries would be declared the winner.

Since those simpler days, the value of a try has slowly increased. In the 1886 revision to the rules, tries became worth one point in and of themselves. This doubled to two points in 1891. Three years later, a try became worth three points, making it more valuable than a conversion for the first time. In 1971, an inflationary period in both economics and sport, the value of the try rose to four points, then five points per try was implemented in 1992.

The reason that they are still called tries is because it's a nice, short, easy word that's relatively simple to say with your mouth full of mud, grass and someone else's leg. There's never been a reason to change it, so why try?

> **The first International match to award five points for a try was between Australia and New Zealand, in July 1992. Australia won 16-15 thanks to a late penalty goal, but Va'aiga Tuigamala had the honour of scoring the first five-point try in the fifth minute. However, both teams scored two tries apiece so the new scoring system made no difference to the outcome of the game.**

· A LITTLE BOOK OF RUGBY ·

> "We want to win, we want to play the game the way we play – hard-hitting, new, exciting, attacking stuff and test it out against the top teams in the world."

England's Sarah Bern explains the appeal of the Rugby World Cup and why the Red Roses are attracting more and more fans.

★ WOMEN'S RUGBY ★

The early history of women's rugby was not very well reported or recorded, and most of the information we have about it comes from secondary sources. They show that women were playing the game almost as soon as it was formalised, but there was quite a lot of public outcry against women playing a full contact sport and, as a result, there is almost more information about games being cancelled because of crowd unrest than there is about the games themselves.

World War I led to a surge in the popularity of women's sport generally, but while it was women's soccer that moved into the limelight in many parts of the country, in Wales, up to 10,000 people were showing up to Cardiff Arms Park to watch Cardiff Ladies play Newport Ladies in charity exhibition matches.

Part of the social objection to women playing sports like rugby was that their fragile frames were ill-suited to the types of impact that they would receive in a full contact sport, so it's interesting to note that one of the players at Cardiff Arms Park during the war, 17-year-old Maria Eley, née Evans, went on to reach the magnificent age of 106. Playing rugby doesn't seem to have done her too much harm.

The end of the war and the return of the troops, though, appears to have put an end to women's rugby as a large-scale spectator sport for the next 70 years. While it doesn't seem to have been overtly banned, it certainly didn't receive any active support. It may have been going on down at the local park, but no one was really talking about it.

The profile of the women's game started to rise in the 1960s when a handful of universities around the world started to put teams together. By the 1980s, a growing number of women's rugby unions were creating and managing national structures.

This led inexorably to discussions about bringing these unions together to form an international competition. This sort of happened in 1990 when New Zealand hosted what was called RugbyFest – a two-week celebration of women's rugby that featured a four-way competition between the Netherlands, New Zealand, the USA and the USSR. Astonishingly, the hosts won the tournament and then beat a combined World XV for dessert, because, well, New Zealand.

This prologue led to the first world cup the following year in Wales. The reason for the lack of capitals in 'world cup' back there is that it was not sanctioned or officially supported by the world rugby authorities. Twelve teams took part, with the USA emerging as the eventual winner.

The tournament may not have been officially sanctioned, but that doesn't mean that it was entirely unsupported. It was organised on a very tight budget, didn't sell television rights and needed to offer financial support to the team from the USSR, which had been unable to bring any hard currency to Wales because the USSR was in the midst of doing its impression of a geopolitical soufflé after someone opened the oven door too early. As a result, the 1991 world cup made a financial loss, although this was recouped by the support of several local businesses and donations at the end of it all from England's RFU.

The second world cup in 1994 nearly didn't go ahead at all, but the fact that it was pulled together at very late notice – after the original hosts had to pull out – showed rugby's governing bodies that the game had passionate support and the potential to become an important part of the rugby community.

Since then, the sport has gone from strength to strength. With the support of the sport's governing bodies around the world, the women's game has become a key component of rugby's growth plans for the next few years.

• A LITTLE BOOK OF RUGBY •

"I'd like to thank the press from the heart of my bottom."

Nick Easter after England defied the odds with their quarter-final win over Australia.

· A LITTLE BOOK OF RUGBY ·

★ SARAH HUNTER ★
(ENGLAND)

Sarah Hunter is England's most capped female player, representing the team at four world cups. Over the course of her international career, she made 141 appearances, won the Six Nations 10 times (nine as grand slams) and was part of the team that won the World Cup in 2014.

Hunter was the face of the women's game as it moved from niche interest to very visible part of the sporting spectrum. She played her first game in an England shirt as an amateur in a Six Nations match against Scotland in front of a half-full stadium with a capacity of 1,000. 16 years later, her final match, having become professional four years previously, was also against Scotland in the Six Nations, but this time in front of a sell-out crowd in a stadium that can host more than 10,000 people. What didn't change was England won both matches.

She started out playing Rugby League as a nine-year-old before switching codes and starting to build her reputation as one of the sport's greatest players. She went on to captain the England side 85 times – the third-highest number of times a player in world rugby, male or female, has pulled on their country's armband (Italy's Sergio Parisse and New Zealand's Richie McCaw captained their national sides 93 and 110 times respectively). She captained England 11 times at a World Cup, matching Will Carling's and Martin Johnson's achievement for England and only being surpassed by Farah Palmer (12) and Richie McCaw (13), both of New Zealand.

"Sport does teach you that and it is not always about being the best you can be or the highest level, it is just doing something you enjoy and working hard at it," says Sarah Hunter. To be fair, she did play to the very highest level, but also enjoyed it and worked very hard.

> **Although most people think women rugby players are professional, like their male counterparts, very few are. Most female players are balancing a full-time career alongside their playing commitments. The England women's rugby team finally received full-time contracts in 2019 for the first time, making them the first international team in the world to go fully professional.**

• A LITTLE BOOK OF RUGBY •

"She is England's greatest player, without a shadow of a doubt. Men's, women's, I can't see how anyone can say there has been a better player."

England head coach Simon Middleton describes Sarah Hunter as her career came to a close in 2023.

★ RUGBY BOOTS ★

Rugby boots have followed a fairly simple design route. They started out as either standard work boots — often complete with steel toecaps and the subtlety and control of a 1970s prop forward given the keys to a brewery — or gentlemen's walking boots. As the game became more formalised, people started to screw iron bars across the soles of their boots to give them a bit of grip.

The very first rules of rugby, written in 1845, had actually stated that boots were not allowed to have nails projecting from the bottom or iron plates on the heels or soles, which tends to conjure up some fairly hair-raising images of the kinds of injuries that were being inflicted in the early days of the sport. It's therefore worth raising a glass in the direction of whoever it was who found the key to creating traction without creating an offensive weapon (mostly).

Even with the rules in place, though, it is said that enterprising rugby players would take their boots down to the local cobbler and have the tips of the nails — sorry, studs — sharpened so that they could inflict that little bit more damage during the game.

Hacking was a perfectly acceptable part of the sport during those early days.

The first major breakthrough came in around the 1890s with the addition of leather studs to offer traction on muddy rugby fields. The quality of the leather used in boots continued to improve during the 20th century, but there wasn't necessarily a significant focus on boots because the kicking game is mostly secondary.

By the 1980s, synthetic materials started to replace leather, and as the sport made its inevitable march towards professionalism, more and more rugby players started wearing football boots, which has at least made the rugby pitch a more colourful place for the first five minutes of a match before everything's caked in mud.

· A LITTLE BOOK OF RUGBY ·

★ MARTIN JOHNSON ★
(ENGLAND)

The Rugby World Cup was first played back in 1987, and since that first tournament, only one team from the northern hemisphere has lifted the Webb Ellis Trophy: England, in 2003, under the leadership of the indomitable Martin Johnson.

With the exception of a couple of summers making the most of the rugby season on the other side of the world by playing with New Zealand's King Country, Johnson stayed with the Leicester Tigers for his entire career, often playing alongside his brother. He made 362 appearances in total and helped them win the Premiership five times (in 1994/95, 1998/99, 1999/2000, 2000/01, 2001/02), the Heineken Cup twice (in 2001 and 2002) and the Pilkington Cup twice (in 1993 and 1997).

He captained the Lions two times, winning the 1997 tour of South Africa but doing the other thing in 2001 in Australia. He also took part in the New Zealand tour in 1993, which was another tour where the Lions did the thing that isn't winning.

With England, Johnson won the Five/Six Nations five times in 1995, 1996, 2000, 2001, 2003, claiming the Triple Crown in 1995, 1996, 1997, 1998, 2002 and 2003, and the Grand Slam in both 1995 and 2003.

Johnson stepped up to the captaincy in 1999 and held on to the armband for 39 matches. When his playing days were behind him he became head coach of England, winning the Six Nations in 2011.

Prior to rugby becoming professional, Johnson worked for Midland Bank (now part of HSBC). At 2.01 m tall (6 foot 7 inches in old money) it's difficult to imagine anyone arguing with him when he turned down a loan.

> The very first game of the first Rugby World Cup was played on May 22, 1987. It was, with respect to the Azzurii, a somewhat one-sided event between New Zealand and Italy that was largely forgettable, aside from an amazing 70-metre try scored by John Kirwan. New Zealand romped home 70-6.

• A LITTLE BOOK OF RUGBY •

"Rugby may have many problems, but the gravest is undoubtedly that of the persistence of summer."

Chris Laidlaw, All Blacks legend, sums up the feelings of millions of rugby enthusiasts around the world.

★ THE BREAK FROM LONDON ★

It's easy to simplify the schism between rugby league and rugby union as an argument about getting paid, but actually it was a little more nuanced than that.

Basically, the clubs in the north-west weren't necessarily arguing in favour of professionalism, but they felt that players deserved to be compensated for their time – and often needed support with any medical bills that arose as a result of playing the sport. Some clubs began to offer so-called 'broken time' payments so that players could afford to play rugby and still put food on the table. This was seen by some of the sport's governing authorities not as professionalism itself, but as a gateway to professionalism.

Adding to the tension was the suggestion by the clubs across Cheshire, Lancashire and Yorkshire that the RFU was dominated by representatives from southern clubs and that it was difficult for representatives to get to meetings from t'north if the meetings were always held in London. History doesn't record whether northern representatives were reimbursed for any meetings in London that they did attend, but it does show that the RFU voted against a proposal for broken time payments in 1893.

This lit the touchpaper and two years later, in 1895, 20 clubs broke away from the RFU to form the Northern Rugby Football Union. Plenty of other teams followed suit over the next few years, particularly after the RFU's edict that any team — even if they were amateur — playing against one of the breakaway teams was guilty of professionalism and would be banned. This made finding games more difficult for some teams, particularly in the north, so they became part of the league simply to get a game. The new sport made the leap to New Zealand in 1905 and then to Australia.

The northern game set up leagues and played for cups similar to football, so people started talking about playing or watching either the league or the union to differentiate between the two sports, and in 1922, the organisation changed its name to Rugby League.

From schism came divergence, and rugby league has developed into very much its own thing over the intervening century.

· A LITTLE BOOK OF RUGBY ·

★ DAN CARTER ★
(NEW ZEALAND)

Dan Carter scored 20 points in his debut test for the All Blacks in 2003, setting the template for a glorious 12 years of international rugby. Looking back over his career, he seems to have taken apart virtually every team he faced. Thirty-three points against the Lions in 2005, back-to-back World Cup champions in 2011 and 2015, Tri Nations and Rugby Championship winner in 2003, 2005, 2006, 2007, 2008, 2010, 2012, 2013 and 2014 and a key part of the team that held the Bledisloe Cup every year between 2003 and 2015.

He played for the All Blacks 112 times between 2003 and 2015, winning 88% of his matches and amassing a humungous 1,598 points – more than any other player in history and 300 more points than the second-highest scorer in Test history. In total, he scored 29 tries, 293 conversions (world record), 281 penalties (world record), and eight drop goals. He also holds the record for points scored against Australia (366) England (178), France (163) and South Africa (255).

When he retired, New Zealand lost one of the most complete rugby players ever to have graced the game. The rest of the world breathed a quiet sigh of relief.

★ BLEDISLOE CUP ★

The Bledisloe Cup is awarded to the winners of a Test between Australia and New Zealand. It started out in either 1931 or 1932 depending on who you believe. The controversy (such as it is) appears to revolve around an alleged match that might have taken place between the two teams in 1931 that no one has any records of, except for a brief reference in the minutes of a meeting of the New Zealand rugby authorities. Weirdly, the New Zealand perspective is that a mention in their own minutes doesn't count, so their official records begin with a three-match series in 1932 while the Australians very graciously suggest that the mythical single match is the start date.

There's probably never going to be an answer about who is correct, and the simple truth is that it doesn't really matter. The reality for the rest of the world is that when Australia and New Zealand want to clash about rugby, the last place you want to be is caught in the middle – although if they don't come to an agreement soon, there's going to be a slightly weird couple of years with Australia celebrating the centenary of the Bledisloe

Cup in 2031 and New Zealand celebrating it a year later. Perhaps they'll recycle the promotional material.

It's also worth pointing out that the two teams have had a strong rugby rivalry dating back to 1903, so the actual date that His Excellency The Right Honourable The Lord Bledisloe, GCMG, KBE, PC, fourth Governor General of New Zealand, came along and stuck a big silver trophy and his name on the competition is kind of incidental.

The trophy has been contested in many different ways over the years, but these days it's mostly a three-match series (dropping to two matches in World Cup years) and has been known to bring in sizable crowds. In 2000, a record-breaking 109,874 people are said to have made their way to watch the two teams slug it out at Sydney's Stadium Australia, which has also gone down in history as 'The Greatest Game of Rugby Ever Played'.

• A LITTLE BOOK OF RUGBY •

"You're not going to please everyone, but then, it's not about pleasing people, it's about winning rugby games."

Wales' Alun Wyn Jones takes a refreshingly honest approach to the art of rugby.

THE BRITISH & IRISH LIONS

Rugby's existence as an amateur or semi-professional sport up until 1995 had some unusual ramifications, one of which was the formation of the British & Irish Lions. The first Lions tour in 1888 was a completely commercial venture that had nothing to do with rugby's governing authorities. Basically, a group of rugby players fancied a holiday in the southern hemisphere and played a bit of rugby while they were at it.

That first tour went around Australia and New Zealand, playing 35 matches against local sides but without facing off against either of the national sides. Three years later, South Africa got in on the act, inviting a 'British Isles' team to come south and play 17 matches against local opposition and three Test matches.

This carried on for a while, but in 1924 there were two changes that set the tour apart. Firstly, the team adopted the four-quartered shield on their shirt, which brings together the four represented rugby unions and is still used today (with modern flourishes). The team also wore ties bearing a lion rampant while they were out and about on tour business (other than when playing), and the press started referring to them as the 'Lions' for the first time.

There was quite a bit of controversy about the Lions' tour of New Zealand in 1930 because the tourists' dark blue jerseys forced the All Blacks to play in a changed strip, so when they next visited in 1950 as the world recovered from World War II, they switched to a red shirt, white shorts, blue socks with green turnovers that they have worn ever since. Materials have changed, sponsors have been added (in 1993), but the Lions have stuck with the colour scheme ever since.

These days, being invited on the Lions tour is one of the highest accolades that a British or Irish rugby player can be offered. The tours take place every four years and there's an informal – but relatively strict – rotation of the tours between Australia, South Africa and New Zealand; each is, therefore, visited every 12 years. So it's a big deal when the Lions come to town.

• A LITTLE BOOK OF RUGBY •

"It still has an important place in professional rugby. It's even more important now to have it because everything is so intense, so pressurised and serious. You need to have an opportunity to enjoy rugby for the reasons you started playing for. You just want to pick up the ball and play and have fun."

England's Joe Marler explains the simple attraction of playing for the Barbarians.

Player	Years active
Israel Folau (Australia/Tonga)	2013–present
Jonah Lomu (New Zealand)	1994–2002
Akaki Tabutsadze (Georgia)	2020–present
Serge Blanco (France)	1980–1991
Joost van der Westhuizen (South Africa)	1993–2003
D.T.H. van der Merwe (Canada)	2006–2019
Adam Ashley-Cooper (Australia)	2005–2019
Ben Smith (New Zealand)	2009–2019
Chris Latham (Australia)	1998–2007
Gareth Thomas (Wales/British & Irish Lions)	1995–2007
Beauden Barrett (New Zealand)	2012–present
Jeff Wilson (New Zealand)	1993–2002
Joe Rokocoko (New Zealand)	2003–2010
Christian Cullen (New Zealand)	1996–2002
Julian Savea (New Zealand)	2012–2017
Brian O'Driscoll (Ireland/British & Irish Lions)	1999–2014
George North (Wales/British & Irish Lions)	2010–2024
Doug Howlett (New Zealand)	2000–2007
Rory Underwood (England/British & Irish Lions)	1984–1996)
Hirotoki Onozawa (Japan)	2001–2013
Shane Williams (Wales/British & Irish Lions)	2000–2011
David Campese (Australia)	1982–1996
Bryan Habana (South Africa)	2004–2016
Daisuke Ohata (Japan)	1996–2006

· A LITTLE BOOK OF RUGBY ·

★ MOST TEST TRIES ★

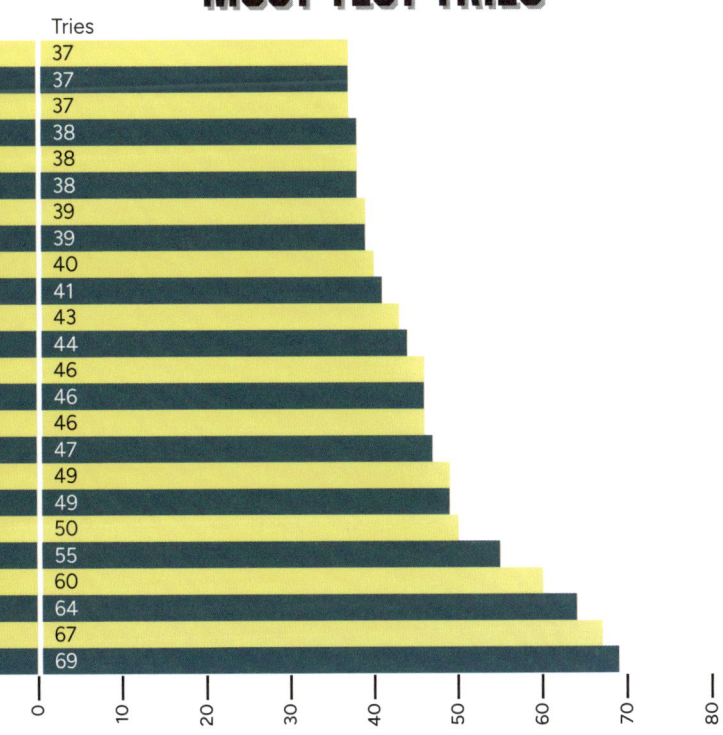

Tries
37
37
37
38
38
38
39
39
40
41
43
44
46
46
46
47
49
49
50
55
60
64
67
69

0 — 10 — 20 — 30 — 40 — 50 — 60 — 70 — 80 —

★ THE TOM RICHARDS CUP ★

The Tom Richards Cup is awarded to the winners of a Test series between the British & Irish Lions and Australia. It was created in honour of Australian-born Tom Richards, who is the only Australian to have played for both the Lions and the Wallabies (despite nearly playing for South Africa first. It's a long story involving 1906 selection criteria).

Richards spent a season in England, playing for Bristol before heading back to Australia, where he was selected for the national side between 1908 and 1912, picking up an Olympic gold medal for rugby during the 1908 London Games. In 1910, he was in South Africa when an injury-ravaged Lions squad needed some more players. His season with Bristol meant that he was eligible to be a Lion (long story involving 1910 selection criteria), so Lion he became, making two appearances. By 1912 he was back with Australia, latterly representing them on a tour of the United States and Canada.

British newspaper *The Times* once suggested that he would be the first person on the team sheet if Earth was ever to play Mars. He served at Gallipoli and Arras and won the military cross for gallantry during World War I.

While Richards is the only Australian to have represented both teams, England-born Blair Swannell represented the Lions in 1899 and 1904 before moving to Australia in 1905, making a single appearance for the Wallabies.

The cup that's named in Richards' honour was commissioned for the 2001 Lions tour of Australia and has so far been won by Australia once and the Lions once. Bring on 2025.

Australia won the first Tom Richards Cup 2-1 in 2001, when captain John Eales was presented with the inaugural trophy at Sydney's Stadium Australia. In 2013, the Lions regained their pride by winning 2-1, again in Australia.

· A LITTLE BOOK OF RUGBY ·

★ BRYAN HABANA ★
(SOUTH AFRICA)

Bryan Habana made his Test debut against England in 2004, coming off the bench to score a try with his first touch, catching hold of a fast-paced pass, running through tackles down the left wing and placing it neatly between the sticks. It was the world's first taste of his lethal finishing and he quickly became a pivotal part of South Africa's rugby team for the next 12 years.

He made 124 Test appearances for the Springboks, making 335 points during that time and challenging records set by Jonah Lomu a decade before.

Speed, exceptional footwork and a keen eye for an opportunity marked him out as a player. In 2007, he helped South Africa win their second World Cup and Habana found himself named the International Rugby Board's Player of the Year in the process. The tournament saw him equal Lomu's record of eight tries in a World Cup (a record that is now split three ways with New Zealand's Julian Savea). In 2015, Habana also matched Lomu's record of 15 World Cup tries.

In terms of national games, he won South Africa's premier domestic competition, the Currie Cup, in 2009 with the Blue Bulls, the southern hemisphere's Super Rugby competition with the Bulls in 2007 and 2009. He moved to Toulon in France for the final five years of his playing career, winning the Top 14 in 2014 and the Heineken Cup/European Champions Cup in 2014 and 2015.

He was named after Bryan Robson and Gary Bailey, two greats of the Manchester United football team. Comparing exploits across sports is difficult, but there's little doubt that Habana etched his name indelibly across South African and world rugby.

> The Currie cup, named after Sir Donald Currie, owner of a British shipping company, is held every year and competed in by teams from all over South Africa. In 1891, a British rugby team travelled to South Africa to play against a few local teams, and Currie provided a gold cup for the eventual winners. The format of the cup has changed many times and was not regularly held until 1968.

• A LITTLE BOOK OF RUGBY •

"I'm a great believer in coaching, but I believe in players even more."

English prop Fran Cotton suggests that shouting from the touchlines during the match doesn't always help.

★ FREE FOR ALL AND ALL FOR ONE ★

Lions tours might sound like a bit of a jolly, getting together with a group of like-minded individuals, having a bit of a holiday and dabbling in a spot of rugby, but they are actually hard work. There is a lot of pride that goes with pulling on that particular jersey, and teams from the southern hemisphere are always going to offer a tough contest.

Back in 1974, in the days before professionalism, the Lions headed down to South Africa chasing their first Test victory against the Springboks on tour since 1955. There was a bit of needle between the two teams, because a) there's always a bit of needle, and b) six years earlier, Wales player John O'Shea had become the first Lion to be sent off for foul play after an incident in which fists had been thrown.

According to the boot-room analysis, part of the reason why O'Shea had been sent off was that he had been standing on his own against the opposition, making it easy for the ref to single him out and send him from the field of play. Before the 1974 tour, the Lions looked at the Springboks and saw that they had two advantages: they were physically imposing, and they were good at what is politely called 'off-the-ball play'. Basically, they were big and liked to throw a punch when the ref's back was turned. It's possible that the South Africans had a different perspective on this suggestion, but it's also possible that they'd just smirk, crack their knuckles and maintain eye contact for an uncomfortable length of time.

The decision was made not to be intimidated by the South Africans and that if a Lion squared up to a Springbok or vice versa, the rest of the team would step up and help them stand their ground. The '99 call' was born. If a Lions player got into it, someone would shout "99", and all the Lions players would get into it.

The Lions had won the first two matches through a mixture of sublime rugby and a willingness to respond in kind to any attempts at intimidation. There was a brief pause in hostilities during the second match while players from both sides crawled around on the floor looking for a glass eye that had been knocked out, so rugby's alleged spirit of chivalry wasn't completely lost, but in the main, they were very physical matches.

When the third Test rolled around, everyone was expecting some pushback from the Boks, who basically decided that they weren't going to stand for the Lions not standing for it. Push back they did. Fists flew. Players were running half-way up the pitch to deliver off-the-ball retribution. It wasn't a match; it was an unedifying 80-minute brawl that looked more like calcio storico fiorentino than rugby (see page 46).

It was, by all accounts, an ugly afternoon, and one that makes the responsible adults in the room glad that these days there are video referees to (mostly) put a stop to that sort of thing. The Lions won the series – the first time that had been achieved in South Africa in the 20th century – and nearly made it a clean sweep but for a controversially disallowed try in the final moments of the last Test. The team has gone down in history as one of the greatest that the British Isles has ever put together.

"Barbarian Rugby is about a feeling, I think; or an essence; or a soul to the game."

New Zealand's Wilson Whineray might be talking about the philosophy of Barbarian rugby or trying to advertise a perfume.

· A LITTLE BOOK OF RUGBY ·

★ GAVIN HASTINGS ★
(SCOTLAND)

Gavin Hastings was synonymous with Scottish rugby from the mid-1980s to his retirement in 1995. Often playing alongside his brother Scott, Hastings earned 61 caps for Scotland during that time, 20 of them as captain. He scored 17 international tries, although most of the 667 points that he amassed came with the boot, which was a fearsome weapon that rarely let Scotland down (with the exception of that one time during the 1991 World Cup semi-final when the English commentators cursed it by suggesting that Hastings wouldn't miss because he was too good and playing too well). His points total was a Scottish record until it was surpassed by Chris Paterson in 2008.

He was part of three British & Irish Lions teams — firstly against a Rest of the World XV in 1986, then against Australia in 1989, before taking the captain's armband in 1993 for a tour in New Zealand.

When he retired he had a brief dalliance with American football, unsurprisingly playing as a placekicker (the bloke who does the kicking). He scored 24 of his 27 conversion attempts with his team the Scottish Claymores, winning World Bowl VI in front of nearly 40,000 fans in Edinburgh.

★ THE CALCUTTA CUP ★

The Calcutta Cup is contested each year between England and Scotland during the annual Six Nations Championship. It's been part of rugby's fixture list every year since 1879, with only a handful of interruptions. Two of these were for periods during the world wars, once in 1885 because England and Scotland weren't speaking to each other after an argument about refereeing their 1884 meeting, and then again in 1888 and 1889 when England was excluded for refusing to join the International Rugby Football Board.

As the name suggests, the cup was created in India in the city now called Kolkata. On Christmas Day 1872 (although it might have been 1871) a game of rugby broke out between two groups of soldiers representing England and Scotland. This led to the formation of the Calcutta Rugby Football Club by a group of expats (some of whom had been educated at a private school in, yes, you guessed it, Warwickshire), but by 1878 the club was struggling for players. This may or may not have had something to do with the ending of the free bar that is said to have been a catalyst of the club's initial success. Its final act as a going concern was to take its last 270 Indian rupees out of the bank, and use them to create a trophy.

Said trophy, 45 cm tall with three king cobra handles and an elephant on top, was presented to the RFU, who decided to award it to winners of matches between England and Scotland. There have now been more than 130 such meetings, which currently take place at Murrayfield on even years and Twickenham on odd years.

England have the bragging rights having won the encounter just over 55% of the time. Scotland have won just over a third of the time, but are on for a five-year unbeaten streak if they can get past England at Twickenham in 2025; this is a feat that Scotland has never achieved in the history of the competition. (England have achieved it five times in 1920–24 (5 consecutive matches), 1951–57 (7), 1991–99 (9), 2001–05 (5) and 2011–17 (7)).

· A LITTLE BOOK OF RUGBY ·

★ GEORGE GREGAN ★
(AUSTRALIA)

One of the best ways to announce your arrival on the international rugby scene is to make a match-saving tackle against an All Black who is careering, seemingly inevitably, towards the try line. George Gregan did just this in 1994, putting in a perfectly placed tackle on Jeff Wilson that dislodged his hold on the ball just as he stretched for the line. It was a move that preserved a hard-fought Australian lead that had narrowed to a single point as the second half of the match had progressed.

Gregan relished the opportunities to face off against the neighbours from over the Tasman Sea, lifting the Bledisloe Cup six times in 1994, 1998, 1999, 2000, 2001 and 2002. He played for Australia 139 times in total, making him the sixth-most capped player in rugby history.

His 1994 tackle gained him the respect of Australian rugby fans, but an on-field comment caught by cameras at the end of the Australia–New Zealand World Cup semi-final in 2003 made Gregan an out-and-out legend. Just as the whistle went, the victorious Wallabies captain surveyed the All Blacks who were being sent home without the trophy and said simply: "That's four more years, boys. Four more years."

Gregan played most of his club rugby with Canberra's Brumbies, winning the Super Rugby competition with them in 2001 and

2004. He also turned out for Rugby Club Toulonnais (Toulon) in France and Suntory Sungoliath in Japan. When his retirement was announced, a stand at the Brumbies' Canberra Stadium was renamed in honour of Gregan and longstanding teammate Stephen Larkham's contributions to the club. While sledging is usually reserved for the cricket pitch and rarely saved for the end of the match, the relish with which Gregan delivered the line is difficult to fault.

He had form as a wind-up merchant though. In 2004 the Lions were within a mane hair's breadth of taking the series against Australia. In the final moments of the final match, they were pushing the Wallabies hard and looked like they might be about to grab the handful of points they needed for a famous victory. The Australians were stretched, but a pass went loose, Andrew Walker snaffled up the ball and made his way calmly to the line to put the match out of the Lion's reach. Gregan was standing nearby, held up the first two fingers of his right hand to his lips, and blew the smoke from his imaginary gun. Do Lions growl? They did that day.

• A LITTLE BOOK OF RUGBY •

> "Looking back, my whole life seems so surreal. I didn't just turn up on the doorstep playing rugby; I had to go through a whole lot of things to get there."

Jonah Lomu reflects on the years of hard work that made him a legend.

★ THE BARBARIANS ★

The Barbarians Football Club, also known as the Barbarians, furthermore known as the Baa-Baas, are an invitational team put together to face off against any teams that happen to wander by unawares. The male side was set up in 1890, with a women's team joining the fun in 2017.

And fun really is the emphasis. It's a team made up of players from all over the world, coming together to share their flare and passion for the sport, playing expansive rugby with a smile on their faces as they hunt for points.

Like so many great ideas, the original concept emerged after a late supper, in this case at Bradford's renowned Leuchters Restaurant. William Percy Carpmael, a Victorian gentleman and owner of an inevitably phenomenal pair of immaculately coiffured moustaches, decried the fact that spring would soon arrive to put an end to his beloved rugby season. He decided to set up a touring rugby team formed of players of good spirit – both on and off the field – who would go around the country and take on the best teams at the end of the season.

It was what can only be described as a really nice idea, giving players who were usually opponents, either at club or national level, the chance to play together and finish the season with a flourish. It's a concept that is still relished nearly 135 years later.

The team plays in black and white hooped jerseys, black shorts and the player's home team's socks, which is why the scrums always looks so odd. They played with a menacing skull and crossbones motif in their first season, but this was softened to the club's initials intertwined after 1891 – a banner that they play under to this day.

They also traditionally have at least one uncapped player among their ranks, although there is a lot of competition for the honour of being seen as good enough for a place on a Barbarians side, so it's not a hard and fast rule. In terms of the men's game, players from more than 30 countries have pulled on a Baa-Baa's shirt, and the team has played in more than 25 countries around the world.

The Final Challenge against the Barbarians is traditionally the last game played by an Australia, New Zealand or South Africa side that has toured Britain and Ireland. The first Final Challenge was played in 1948 in Wales and was intended to help raise the funds to get a touring Australian side home (via Canada). 45,000 rugby fans turned up to watch the match, and a new tradition was forged.

★ GAELIC FOOTBALL ★

One game that has some of its roots steeped in Rugby is Gaelic football. Ireland had similar traditions of mob football to most other countries of western Europe and when rugby started to be codified in the 1860s, some parts of the country took to the emerging game, others took more to football, and local games, tending to be known collectively as 'caid', held sway elsewhere.

There was a lot of social change at the time, with people leaving Ireland to seek their fortune around the world, and it appears that they bumped into various other versions of rugby and football while they were out and about.

Some of this diaspora came back, some having made a fortune, some less so, and brought with them accounts of different games being organised in different ways in different parts of the world. These codes started to come together, mingle with traditional Irish field games and become what is today called Gaelic football, which is why it bears some similarities to lots of different sports while at the same time is very much its own thing.

> **"If the game is run properly as a professional game, you do not need 57 old farts running rugby,"**
>
> said England captain Will Carling in a widely reported off-record comment.

· A LITTLE BOOK OF RUGBY ·

★ JONAH LOMU ★
(NEW ZEALAND)

The unstoppable Jonah Lomu arrived on the rugby scene at the perfect time. Money was starting to flow into the game after its move to professional status in 1995 and Lomu's strength, power, size and grace quickly made him the sport's first global superstar.

He was tall and built like a brick outhouse, but he was fast with it: whenever you think of him, he's carving through defences like a knife through butter, defenders either missing him entirely, bouncing off him or clinging to his leg in a desperate, and generally futile, attempt to slow down his inexorable movement towards the line. Unless you were one of the 15 opposition players trying to make the tackle, it was a wonderous sight.

He came into the world's consciousness during the 1995 World Cup, effortlessly putting four tries past England in the semi-finals, although despite his heroics, it was South Africa that lifted the cup that year. Despite never winning the World Cup, he jointly holds the record for the most tries scored in the tournament alongside Bryan Habana, with 15 tries in 11 games.

Lomu quickly evolved into a global sports brand, with McDonalds renaming a burger after him in New Zealand and a couple of computer games published with his name and image plastered all over them. He was a big draw wherever he went.

Health issues related to a kidney disorder shortened his career, and while he came back from a kidney transplant in 2004, he didn't play internationally again. He died at the age of 40 of a heart attack related to his health issues.

In many ways, the fact that he changed rugby in such a short period of time only emphasises his legacy as a player. At the risk of oversimplifying it: before Lomu, wingers tended to be fast and agile; after Lomu, wingers have tended to become fast, agile and big.

> It is said that back in 2001, the company that owned both union's Leeds Tykes and league's Leeds Rhinos put in a third bid for Lomu that would have enabled him to play both codes of the sport. Quite where he would have found time for a holiday in the midst of all that is anyone's guess.

★ WHY SING THE ★ NATIONAL ANTHEM?

The singing of the national anthems is now an accepted pre-match ritual before international matches in many sports, but the roots of the tradition can be traced back to a rugby match in 1905 between New Zealand and Wales.

The first New Zealand touring squad to journey out of Australasia, known as the Original All Blacks, came to western Europe that year and had beaten Ireland, Scotland and England while on their travels before they faced Wales. So basically, there was quite a lot of pride on the line.

According to the history books, the All Blacks performed their haka to a respectful crowd, but once it had concluded, the Welsh team led the 47,000 spectators at Cardiff Arms Park in a spontaneous and rousing rendition of Hen Wlad Fy Nhadau ('Land of My Fathers').

A tradition was born. By 1924, the Olympic Games started playing national anthems to honour gold medal winners; from there, increasing numbers of major sporting events adopted the practice in the years following.

Wales won the 1905 match, by the way, romping home to a 3–0 victory (using the early scoring system (see page 59).

A hundred and odd years later, and the 2023 Rugby World Cup got off to a controversial start for some when the French organisers decided to forgo the usual rousing versions of the various national anthems in favour of having pre-recorded children's choirs take the honour.

It was a decision that had ... repercussions. Right from the word go, there was a lot of stuff spouted on social media about how it took away the dignity of the national anthems which were, after all, an invention of the New Zealand rugby team back in 1905, but really the problem wasn't that the choirs were doing a particularly bad job.

The issue was more that the organisers tried to do something clever with the anthems that would make people stop and admire them. In many ways this misses the point of the national anthems, which is basically an opportunity for fans to warm their voices up and get their heads together (unless you are drawn against Uruguay which has an anthem that is longer than pretty much every other nation's put together).

Either way, sadly, the anthems for France 2023 were quickly and politely remixed so that the crowds could have a proper sing-song before the actual entertainment started.

Meanwhile, since 1991, the Rugby World Cup has had its own anthem in the form of *The World in Union*. At its heart, it's a version of Gustav Holst's *Thaxted*, a tune he wrote in honour of the town in Essex where he lived most of his life, with some lyrics about niceness, togetherness and everybody getting along and stuff.

Holst developed the tune from an original melody that he'd included in his seminal *Planets* suite – in *Jupiter, Bringer of Jolity*, to be specific. It was originally supposed to be used as a tune to accompany the poem *I vow to thee my country*, which is why it often pops up at various ceremonial events as a result.

In its *World in Union* form, it is usually brushed down before every tournament and given a gloss of each host nation's cultural references. Interestingly, Swedish extreme metal band Balthory also delivered a version of the tune in 1991 called *Hammerheart*, although in this form it was more interested in the inevitable twilight of gods that had sacrificed an eye for wisdom rather than unity and new dawns. Although they might have been singing about the 1974 Lions tour of South Africa – it's a little difficult to tell.

★ GIL EVANS' WHISTLE ★

That 1905 New Zealand tour was the start of a quite a few things, it seems. If you listen closely to the start of a Rugby World Cup between 1987 and 2015, you'll hear the dulcet tones of Gil Evans' whistle, which was first used 80-odd years before, when England faced New Zealand at Crystal Palace for the first time. The All Blacks won that particular meeting with a comfortable 15 points to zero, mostly because they had allegedly been doing that most un-rugby-like thing and practising line-outs and scrums rather than just bundling about and waiting to see what happened – which is how every other team in the world played at the time. The cads. The bounders.

Gil Evans, the Welsh referee of that day in south London, then gave his whistle to Albert Freethy, who used it to adjudicate the final of the Olympic Games' rugby tournament in 1924 (when the USA beat France to take gold). Freethy then used the whistle again in 1925 during a clash between England and New Zealand. It was used in the eighth minute to send off All Black forward Cyril Brownlie. This was actually a big deal because it made Brownlie the first rugby player to be sent off during a match.

Despite being a man down, the Kiwis still won the match with 17–11.

After many adventures and a long and storied career, in 1969, the whistle put its kit in a bag and made its way to New Zealand to set up home on the shelves of a rugby museum in the city of Palmerston North.

It then came out of retirement in 1987, and was used for the opening of the Rugby World Cup in New Zealand. It continued to be used for the opening of every World Cup up until 2015, when it was felt that it was getting a little long in the tooth.

> **"Rugby is a game for barbarians played by gentlemen. Football is a game for gentlemen played by barbarians,"**

suggested Oscar Wilde. Winston Churchill, meanwhile, stood right next to the line of copyright infringement when he suggested: "Rugby is a hooligans' game played by gentlemen."

THE FREETHY FLORIN

The second sacred relic of rugby, the Freethy florin, made its first appearance at the game between England and New Zealand in 1925. At the start of the match, referee Albert Freethy realised he didn't have a coin to toss, and neither did either of the two captains (which is not massively surprising really because most rugby players travel light on the pitch), so he turned to a nearby New Zealand supporter, Hector Gray, and blagged him for a bit of spare change.

Gray obliged, and was so overjoyed at being able to help out the match officials, he had one side of the coin embossed with a fern and the other with a rose to commemorate New Zealand and England – in flagrant disregard of rules about defacing the currency. Like Gil Evans' whistle (see previous page), the coin ambled its way through history and has been used for the coin toss at the start of the Rugby World Cup since 1987.

★ RUGBY SCHOOL ALSO ★ RESPONSIBLE FOR AUSSIE RULES

History's a funny old thing, and occasionally it throws up random nuggets that are of absolutely no value until you end up in a pub quiz with a very specific question. Case in point: the creator of Aussie rules football, more correctly identified as Aussie rules, was actually an alumnus of Rugby School.

Tom Wills – or to give him his full title, Thomas Wentworth Wills – grew up in the Australian bush, where he is said to have befriended and learned the customs of local Aboriginal tribes. In 1849, when he was 14, he was shipped off to Rugby School, where he was presumably encouraged to keep the local Warwickshire tribes safely at arm's length. While he was being educated at the school, he is said to have played early versions of the eponymous game, and even captained the school team. He was also a keen cricketer, again captaining the school team and later turning out for both Kent and the Marylebone Cricket Club.

He returned to Australia and continued to play cricket, but decided that he wanted to do something to stay active during the winter months. He started the process of developing Aussie Rules based on his memory of the games that he played at Rugby School but adapting them for the hotter, drier local conditions. This means that Rugby School is directly responsible for two different codes of the sport.

> Aussie rules football – better known in some parts of the world as AFL – remains one of Australia's most widely watched sports – and it is growing in popularity worldwide. Although it is sort of originally based on rugby, throwing the ball is outlawed. Players can kick the ball to a player if they are more than 15 metres away, and if that target player catches the ball without it touching the ground, they earn a mark. A mark is rather like a penalty, in that it earns the team a free kick.

· A LITTLE BOOK OF RUGBY ·

★ GARETH EDWARDS ★
(WALES)

Rugby union's decision to switch from amateur to professional has understandably led to a quantum leap in training, levels of fitness, recovery from injury and the number of games played; as a result, most of the leading players of the sport have come from the modern era.

No list of rugby's greats is complete without Gareth Edwards, though. He first played for the Welsh national side at 19 and became its youngest captain a year later.

Rugby is an intense game and as a player you need time to recover both physically and mentally from a tough match, particularly at international level. Despite this, Edwards has described being able to go to work for the first half of the week as wonderful when Wales won, because everyone was on a high.

So, it's just as well that Edwards stood at the heart of a phenomenal Welsh team that dominated European rugby, enjoying an 11-year career that started in 1967 and concluded 53 caps later in 1978. Edwards helped Wales win the Five Nations Championship in 1969 (with a Triple Crown), share the honours with France in 1970, win it outright with a Grand Slam in 1971 (with a Triple Crown on top), win it again in 1975 and take the Grand Slam and Triple Crown again in both 1976 and 1978. Yes, winning a Grand Slam means that you've won the Triple Crown by default, but it's still a feat worth mentioning. Wales also won the Triple Crown in 1977 but lost out on the overall title to France.

Edwards also played 10 times for the British & Irish Lions, including on the legendary (/notorious) tour of South Africa in 1974 (see page 94). A year before, playing for the Lions against the All Blacks, he delivered what has become known as 'That Try': an exceptional, almost telepathic, achievement with his teammates, tearing through the Kiwis and exemplifying what the Lions team is supposed to be about. How do you take a pass at that speed, hold on to it, accelerate and then take it past that many All Blacks to find the line?

By being very, very good.

★ IS RUGBY SCHOOL ★ ALSO RESPONSIBLE FOR AMERICAN FOOTBALL?

Rugby School broadly created rugby and had a strong influence on the rise of Aussie rules, but sadly there the streak ends. American football might well have taken some initial inspiration from the sport, but there's little evidence of any Rugby School alumni playing a direct role in the development of Gridiron.

The first game of American football was played between two college teams in 1869 with a spherical ball and no handling. While the sport went on to embrace both the elongated ellipsoidal ball and picking up the ball (the forward pass wasn't legal until 1906), it has always been a different thing.

It was influenced by British sports, such as rugby and football, but native American sports, such as Mohican ball, are also said to have made their way into the mix. Basically, they are not branches of the same tree, but they share a few of the same roots.

★ SPEAK TO ME LIKE THAT AGAIN … ★

Rugby is undoubtedly a complex sport played by people at the very peak of physical fitness (at the top level) that always appears to be teetering on the very edge of becoming a brawl (with the exception of the final Test of the 1974 Lions tour of South Africa, which teetered over the edge of becoming a brawl). So it's right that we take a moment to appreciate the calm reserve that referees exhibit when managing the whole fandango.

Referees are expected to have complete recall of a complex set of rules and enforce them with calm authority against players who are at least twice their size. For generations, the holders of the sacred whistle have stood their ground, kept games moving and held back the rolling tide of barbarism that often seems to have engulfed other team sports. It can be like watching a spaniel put a Doberman in its place – but that's what the referees do, week in, week out.

There are three factors that you need to take into account when it comes to rugby and the role that referees play.

Firstly, the rules are complicated, secondly the game is fast, and thirdly, there can be a lot of mud flying about. Putting those three facts together, it is frankly astonishing that anyone gets 90% of the calls right. At the top level, being able to go upstairs and do the whole TMO thing has changed the dynamic somewhat, but in many ways it's not too surprising that there are those that suggest that a lot of refereeing in rugby is not perhaps about being absolutely correct, it's about being able to deliver your decision with enough authority to convince everyone else you know what you are talking about. A spaniel can put a Doberman in its place if the spaniel really believes that it is right and the Doberman has a scintilla of doubt.

Take a moment to watch a match from the referee's point of view and marvel at the performance of the most important person on the pitch. In the end, you might not always like their decisions, but the game couldn't go on without them.

★ THE TRIPLE CROWN ★

Once upon a time, when the world was very young, rugby was sometimes a quirky sport. One such example of this is the Triple Crown, which is awarded to the team that beats all three of the other home nations in the Six Nations tournament. In many ways it was a hangover from the Home Nations Championship, which preceded the Five Nations Championship, which has in turn been replaced by the current Six Nations Championship.

The Home Nations Championship was first contested in 1883, but the term 'Triple Crown' doesn't appear to have been seen in print until 1894, when it was mentioned in an article in the Irish Times. It may have been used prior to this, but there doesn't seem to be a record of it.

Either way, at the time, if a team beat all of the home nations, they won the Home Nations Championship trophy, making the concept of a Triple Crown trophy superfluous. As a result, it became known as the 'invisible cup': everyone in England, Scotland and Wales wanted to win it – because everyone loves a clean sweep of the neighbours in the championship – but winning it was just bragging rights, not silverware.

This slightly eccentric piece of rugby heritage came to an end in 2006 when some bright spark decided to create a trophy to accompany the Triple Crown, making it a physical thing to strive for after more than a century. It's probably the right thing to recognise the achievement of beating all of the home nations in the tournament, but you can't help but feel it takes away some of the magic of the invisible cup.

Either way, England has won the Triple Crown 26 times, Wales 22 times, Ireland 13 times and Scotland 10 times. Not all of the magic has dissipated: it is still possible to win the Triple Crown and not win the Six Nations, although it surely does help.

· A LITTLE BOOK OF RUGBY ·

★ GARY ARMSTRONG ★
(SCOTLAND)

Gary Armstrong was a stalwart of the Scotland team that delivered a Five Nations Grand Slam in 1990. It was the 13th time that Scotland had lifted the trophy, the 10th time they'd won the Triple Crown and only the third time they'd won the Grand Slam (including the victories in the Home Nations competition that evolved into the Five Nations).

In the final match of the 1990 tournament, it was England that had the momentum. Both England and Scotland were on for the Grand Slam, but the Auld Enemy had brushed aside France, Ireland and Wales, while Scotland's victories had been hard fought, narrow affairs. At the end of the match the teams were matched with a try apiece, but it was the three penalties that England conceded and Scotland scored that were the difference between the two sides and had the Murrayfield crowds jubilantly invading the pitch at the final whistle. And it was Armstrong who had been at the centre of virtually every Scottish move during the match.

By 1999, when Scotland next won the Five Nations, Armstrong was captain, leading the team to another last gasp victory (although this time it was the Welsh that stopped England to hand Scotland the championship).

Armstrong came out of retirement briefly in 2018 at the ripe old age of 51 to play for Stewart's Melville's third XV as a favour for Scotland and Lions teammate Finlay Calder. Rumours are that the Lothians echoed with the sound of creaking the next day.

> It's been suggested that one of the reasons for Scotland's legendary victory in 1990 was that an overzealous England merchandiser started selling t-shirts celebrating England's Grand Slam outside Murrayfield before the match had even kicked off, and when word of this reached the Scottish dressing room, spirits were galvanised.
>
> To be fair, the same thing happened in reverse in 2012. This was in the midst of a winning streak for the English that carried on for another six years.

★ THE COOK CUP/ ★
ELLA-MOBBS TROPHY

The Cook Cup/Ella-Mobbs Trophy is another example of rugby adding a formal trophy to an existing fixture a century after the fixture started to be played. In this case, the Cook Cup was created in 1997, 88 years after England had first faced off against Australia in 1909 at the Rectory Field in Blackheath, south London.

Interestingly, the two teams didn't actually play each other very often in the pre-professional era. It was 19 years before they played again after that first match, another 20 years passed before their next meeting and then another decade after that before the next match. With the rise of the jet-age their meetings started to become more common: the teams met twice in the 1960s, four times in the 1970s, six times in the 1980s and three times in the 1990s before the unveiling of the Cook Cup.

The clash between the two teams has now become a regular feature of the sporting calendar, with the teams regularly welcoming each other on tour. The Cook Cup – named after Captain Cook and, therefore, uncomfortable for Australia's First Nations people – was retired in 2022 in favour of something that slightly better reflected the spirit of the age.

The Ella-Mobbs Trophy that replaced it was named after Australia's Mark Ella and England's Edgar Mobbs.

Ella played for the Wallabies 25 times between 1980 and 1984 and was the first indigenous Australian to captain a national team. He wore the armband 10 times, including during a tour of Britain and Ireland, where Australia beat England, Ireland, Scotland and Wales, and where he scored a try in each match.

Mobbs, meanwhile, made seven appearances for England, scoring during that first match with Australia in 1909. He enlisted for the army in World War I but was killed during the Third Battle of Ypres while trying to take out a machine gun post during a battle that also saw many Australians lay down their lives. Mobbs' body was never found, so he is commemorated on the Menin Gate in Belgium.

★ THE FART THAT ★
CRACKED A MOUNTAIN

By the early 1990s, there had been more than a century of dealing with scandal after scandal in rugby about people allegedly being paid to play. According to some, having the audacity to expect a living wage for putting their bodies on the line in the name of providing entertainment for others went against the sprit of the game. The problem was that it was becoming increasingly clear that other sports were becoming very wealthy and so rugby bowed to the inevitable and declared itself an 'open' game.

The final straw came in 1995, three weeks before the World Cup, when England captain Will Carling was caught off-mic making a less than diplomatic statement about the RFU's general committee.

After Carling had finished an interview and had removed his microphone, he was asked what he thought of the way that rugby was being managed in light of the fact that one of the committee members had suggested the England players were always looking for ways to break the amateur ethic of the sport. In response, Carling candidly referred to the committee as "57 old farts". Unfortunately, the comment was recorded on the interviewer's microphone and was quickly plastered across the newspapers. Despite calling the president of the RFU to apologise (the president was allegedly sipping claret in his London club at the time), Carling was stripped of his captaincy.

It quickly became very clear, though, that the public were behind Carling. Forty-eight hours later, the RFU was forced into a humiliating U-turn, reinstating him and trying to pretend that everything was fine – that the faint whiff was just the manure that was being fed to the roses to keep them strong.

In many ways it was a fuss over nothing, an off-record comment that should not have made it into the public domain, but the fact that it turned into such a storm highlighted how untenable the whole situation was becoming. It was pretty clear that players in many other countries were being paid for their time, which enabled them to train harder and get better at the game. The amateurism of rugby had become widely known as 'shamateurism'. The fact that some on the committee were willing to sack the England captain on the eve of a World Cup suggested that they were more interested in trying to uphold principles rather than enable the England team to carry the nation, live up to its promise and deliver entertaining, competitive rugby.

The problem was always in the gap between the people who could afford to play as a pastime and the people who still loved the game but also deserved to be paid for their performances. As the game grew, the demands on the players increased but the rewards were limited. Rugby league, meanwhile, had signed a lucrative TV deal, so the opportunities for rugby union players to take their skills elsewhere was also getting bigger.

It was increasingly clear that for the growth, maybe even the survival, of the game, rugby had to become professional. And so, at the end of August 1995, rugby was declared to be an 'open' game, with no restrictions on payments or benefits, along the lines of other professional sports.

It's not solved all of the challenges that the sport faces, but it's made it fairer for the players.

· A LITTLE BOOK OF RUGBY ·

★ JASON ROBINSON ★
(ENGLAND)

Several rugby union players had signed on to play rugby league, often in the twilight of their careers, but very few had come the other way. That changed in the mid-1990s when moving to union began to represent a fresh set of challenges rather than a pay cut.

Jason Robinson is an example of this trend. Having played at the very highest level of rugby league, winning the Super League, a handful of Challenge Cups and several other awards, he made the decision to switch codes in 2000. He made his debut for England in the same season, playing in all of England's victorious World Cup campaign matches in 2003 and going on to make 51 appearances. He also turned out for British & Irish Lions tours to Australia and New Zealand in 2001 and 2005.

Robinson had the subtlety to make precise side steps coupled with a devastating turn of speed which meant that he could draw defenders to where he wasn't, and then leave them standing as he raced for the line. His nickname was Billy Whizz – and it's easy to see why.

★ MOUTHGUARDS ★

Back in the day, many rugby players saw having their teeth knocked out as a matter of personal pride: take a knocking, keep on rocking – as it were. Over the last few years, though, players have become more aware of the long-term implications of repeated blows to the head of the kind that are quite common in the sport of rugby.

For a start, it can make you a whole lot less photogenic, which is important in a world of professional endorsements and sponsorship deals.

More importantly, though, the medical profession and the sport are starting to get a stronger idea about the impact that repeated brain injuries can have on players in the long term. There needs to be a way of moving past the 'shrug it off' culture, which tended to pervade all sports a few decades ago, and getting to a place where the cumulative repercussions of repeated brain injuries are recorded and managed more effectively.

In many ways, the move to professionalism has only made the issue more prominent. Without wanting to offend anyone, rugby players in the past tended to have quite a lot of padding. They had jobs outside of rugby so they weren't training all year round. There are also rumours that they tended to enjoy a pint of beer or two after a match. These days, while the beer might still feature, professional and even amateur players are significantly more solid than their forbears, increasing the risk and severity of injuries if you run into them at speed.

This is where the humble mouthguard is playing an increasingly important role in the evolution of the sport. Putting into a mouthguard a microchip that can monitor impacts and send data to a team's medical staff is likely to enhance understanding of how injuries occur and what measures can be put in place to reduce their severity. Players can be yanked (gently) off the pitch if the blows to the head that they've received have gone over a certain threshold, with the decision removed from the player or the playing staff. Some mouthguards even come with a dental warranty, although this presumably comes with a fair amount of small print.

In many ways, it might be the only way that the sport is going to survive in the long term. Particularly if the next generation of rugby players is going to be able to keep chasing down those lucrative modelling contracts. Which is not something that could have been said four decades ago.

Player	Year
Dan Carter (New Zealand)	2003, 2007, 2011, 2015
Michael Lynagh (Australia)	1987, 1991, 1995
Handré Pollard (South Africa)	2015, 2019, 2023
Gavin Hastings (Scotland)	1987, 1991, 1995
Jonny Wilkinson (England)	1999, 2003, 2007, 2011

· A LITTLE BOOK OF RUGBY ·

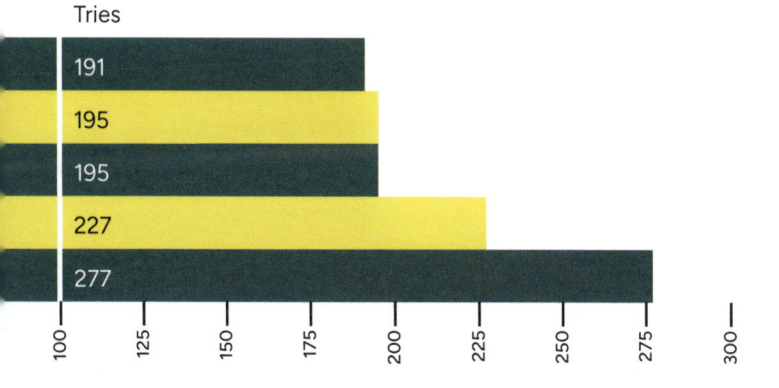

★ WORLD CUP POINTS ★

Tries

191	
195	
195	
227	
277	

100 · 125 · 150 · 175 · 200 · 225 · 250 · 275 · 300

ACCOVACCIARSI, LEGARSI, METTERE IN PAUSA, IMPEGNARSI

While it seems unlikely that calcio storico fiorentino was an influence on the development of rugby (see page 46), is it possible that there's one specific part of rugby that could be influenced by classical Roman strategy?

Back in the day when the Romans were mooching about Europe benignly delivering tomatoes, straightening roads and building hypocaust systems without even asking for anyone's permission, their soldiers developed a system of attack called the testudo, which translates to tortoise, formation. This involved a group of soldiers locking their oblong shields together and moving forward through enemy lines poking folk with short swords through the gaps in the shields as they went. It was a brutally effective form of warfare for the time, was a great way to avoid being peppered with arrows, and underscored why the Roman Army has such a reputation for organisation and innovation. It's part of the reason why celts liked to keep beehives handy because nothing halts the advance of a tortoise full of soldiers in an enclosed space like a swarm of angry bees.

Fast forward a couple of millennia and the scrum is an integral feature of Rugby Union, bringing a group of players together for a great big push-off to see who has the mightiest muscles. Is it possible that a classical scholar at Rugby School was studying their history books, stumbled across the testudo and decided to find a way to integrate it into the game? It would be nice to suggest that this is what happened, but in reality, if you set two teams of teenagers the task of fetching a ball, the chances are that a shoving match will break out whether or not they are classics scholars.

It would be nice to say that the scrum owes a debt of gratitude to the Roman strategies from days of yore, but actually, once again, it's probably just a coincidence.

THE SCRUM

Shirt numbers 1-7 (see page 150) are involved in the scrum, arranged in three rows – front, middle and back. The hooker is in the middle of the front row, and their role is to hook the ball back to the middle row when it is put in. The hooker is flanked by the tighthead and loosehead props, so named because they prop up the whole edifice by leaning in against the opposition props. The easiest way to remember which one goes on which side is of course, lefty loosey, righty tighty.

Holding up the front row are the locks, who literally lock the structure into place. Again, they are tighthead or loosehead depending on whether they are standing on the left or the right.

There was a point where all this was getting a little too simple, so let us turn to the back row. The back row is comprised three players, the outside of which are called flankers. So far so good. In an ideal world, they would be tighthead and loosehead flankers, but that's not where we are, so they are actually called blindside and openside. Blindside is the flanker closest to the touchline while openside has more room to manoeuvre if the opportunity arises.

Finally, there's the number eight, who is crammed in behind the locks and between the flankers. It's the number eight's job to get the ball as it's fed back from the hooker and then make the decision about whether to keep it moving forward at their feet or pick it up and run with it.

The thing is that they are all operating basically blind within the scrum, so they have to rely on information coming in from the players outside to make decisions about what's going on and what to do about it. This is why it's such a team sport.

★ RUGBY AND THE OLYMPICS ★

Rugby's potential relationship with the Olympics is slightly odd, given that while the game's structure is more suited to the summer rather than the winter event, it's a sport that is pretty much designed for the softer ground of the autumn and winter. It doesn't get played in snow and ice (mostly) but it also doesn't get played in the sun (mostly).

Rugby was played at four of the early Olympics after the event was brought back from ancient history at the start of the twentieth century (which is recent rather than ancient history despite what Gen Zs would try to have you believe).

Three teams, France, Germany and Great Britain, chased a gold medal at the Paris games in 1900. This was still in the relatively early days of rugby as an international sport, and the teams that played were teams that happened to be passing rather than what we would consider an international squad these days. France emerged as the winner and the match between France and Britain is said to have had the biggest crowd of the whole Games.

• A LITTLE BOOK OF RUGBY •

The sport skipped the 1904 Olympic Games in the US, but three teams, France, Australasia and Great Britain, did step up for the 1908 Games in Britain. It's all a little weird though; Australasia were represented by an Australian touring team that happened to be in the area, and Great Britain were represented by a team from Cornwall. The French team decided against playing, meaning that the opening match was also the final. Twickenham was still being built so the match was played at the White City stadium, which had the Olympic pool running along side it. As a result, the ball regularly ended up in the drink. Different times.

Rugby skipped the 1912 Olympics, but did make an appearance in 1920 in Belgium. Great Britain declined to send a team and Czechoslovakia and Romania both pulled, out leaving only France and the US to go for gold. The US won.

The US went on to repeat the feat at the 1924 Olympics in Paris, beating France in the final (Romania were the only other nation to field a team). The match was marred by crowd trouble and a pitch invasion that meant that the US team had to be escorted back to their changing room by police. The incident basically marked the end of Union's participation at the Olympic games.

What this means is that the US is the Rugby Union Olympic Champion and has been for over a century. Go figure.

CENTENARY QUAICH TROPHY

Ireland and Scotland tussle for the Centenary Quaich in the Six Nations. Introduced in 1989 to mark the century since the formation of the International Rugby Board (which has subsequently metamorphosised into the World Rugby governing body), it is named after a ceremonial cup that was either used to toast with the water of life, or collect blood.

All in all, it's been contested 36 times, with Ireland enjoying whiskey from the cup around 60% of the time and Scotland enjoying whisky from it around 40% of the time. The match has only been drawn once, back in 1994.

The two teams had been meeting for a long time before someone decided to put a ceremonial cup on it. Their contests started back in 1877 in the Home Nations Cup, and they've played each other competitively more than 140 times since then. Ireland just about hold the bragging rights, winning around half of the time, with Scotland winning just under half of the time. There have only been five draws in all of that history, so you are almost guaranteed to see points scored.

· A LITTLE BOOK OF RUGBY ·

FORWARDS
1. Loose-head prop
2. Hooker
3. Tight-head prop
4. Lock forward
5. Lock forward
6. Blind-side flanker
7. Open-side flanker
8. Number eight

BACKS
9. Scrum-half
10. Fly-half
11. Wing
12. Inside centre
13. Outside centre
14. Wing
15. Full-back

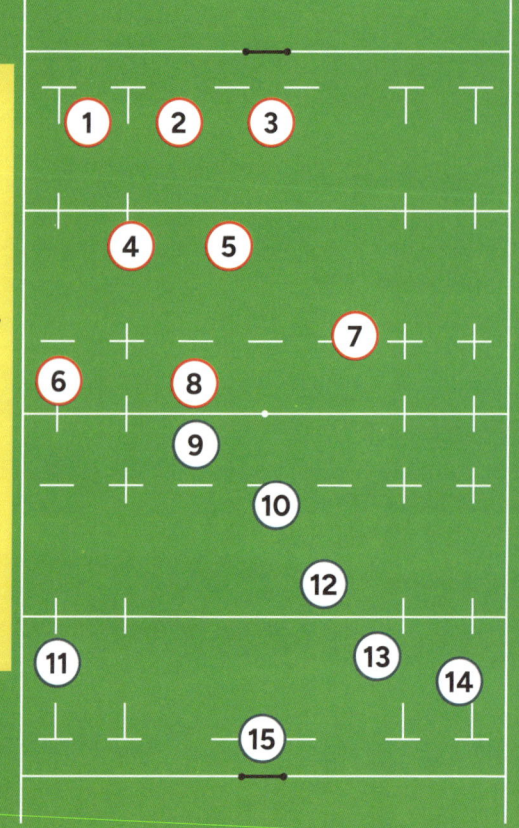

★ WHO GOES WHERE? ★

Rugby and football are basically siblings, and like many siblings, if one does things one way, the other will do it in a completely different way. When it comes to field positions, football focused on simplicity: you either do stuff at the back, stuff in the middle or stuff up front. There's sometimes a touch more nuance than that, but broadly, that's the way football works.

Rugby went the other way, creating precisely defined positions with neatly choreographed roles. There's room for improvisation within that, but basically, when the whistle's about to blow for the start of the match, players know where they should be and what they are about.

In some ways, you might look at this from the outside and think that being so tightly prescriptive could stifle innovation, but in reality rugby's a game of fine margins, where players can find advantage by tiny tweaks, little tucks and, of course, being in the right place to be lucky.

There has also been a change over the last few years. Back in the day, forwards were big, they lumbered towards the opposition flattening them if they got the chance while the people further back tended to be lighter, faster and have significantly better hair so that they looked great as they swooped in, found the hole and took the ball over the tryline.

These days it's changed a bit. Forwards are still big, but many are also far more mobile than they used to be; wingers and backs are still fast but they can also hold their own in the physical stuff. Jona Lomu was probably the catalyst of change. Most coaches in the mid-1990s will have watched him running for the line, completely unhindered by Will Carling and a host of other England stalwarts clinging desperately to his leg, and thought we need bigger, faster, stronger, right across the pitch. Professionalism made it possible.

The positions themselves don't really need to change though, they are comprehensive and give players a shorthand so that they know where they should be on the pitch. How they are doing it though, that will be constantly evolving.

· A LITTLE BOOK OF RUGBY ·

"It's heavier than the wooden spoon,"

reflected Gary Armstong on lifting the Five Nations Trophy in 1999.

· A LITTLE BOOK OF RUGBY ·

★ JONNY WILKINSON ★
(ENGLAND)

Jonny Wilkinson, the man who made it fashionable for kickers to go through the whole weird rigmarole (although to be fair, it clearly worked for him), epitomises the whole 'rugby is a game for barbarians played by gentlemen' cliché. This is a man who trained himself into one of the best fly-halves in the history of rugby and has also delivered lectures on quantum physics while sharing a stage with two Nobel Prize winners. In French.

Wilkinson won 91 caps for England, as well as a further six for the Lions, scoring 1,179 and 67 points, respectively. He helped England win the Six Nations in 2000, 2001, 2003 (with a Grand Slam) and 2011. He also helped win the Triple Crown in 1998, 2002 and 2003. And the World Cup in 2003. Domestically, his Newcastle Falcons won the Premiership in 1997/98 and the Powergen Cup in both 2001 and 2004. He then moved to Toulon and helped them to win the Heineken Cup in 2012/13 and 2013/14, as well as France's Top 14 the same year.

Wilkinson might look like a relative lightweight in comparison to some of his teammates, but Brian O'Driscoll, a man who has, let's face it, exceptional experience, says that the Englishman is responsible for one of the hardest tackles of his career. It happened during the 2003 Six Nations while England were on their way to an eyebrow raising 42–6 victory over Ireland as they warmed up for the World Cup. O'Driscoll was going at full pelt when Wilkinson put in a beautifully timed left-armed tackle that brought the Irishman tumbling down. England turned the ball over and raced up the pitch to find the try line; a winded O'Driscoll had to make his way slowly off the pitch.

Wilkinson first moved away from home to join Newcastle when he was 18. Despite his reputation for meticulous preparation, it is said that he still had to ring his mum before his first trip to the supermarket to check if he needed to take his passport as proof of identification when writing a cheque.

He was probably right to be prepared though; it is also said that when he received his first international call up, again at 18, Jeremy Guscott thought he was in the dressing room as a competition winner rather than a player. If Guscott didn't think he was old enough to play rugby, the supermarket checkout staff would certainly have questioned if he was old enough to be writing cheques. After that World Cup winning kick five years later, people would have been queuing around the block to pay for his shopping. Guscott included.

· A LITTLE BOOK OF RUGBY ·

"Nobody ever beats Wales at rugby. They just score more points."

Legendary All Blacks captain Graham Mourie could have had a career in the diplomatic services.

★ THE MAN IN SEAT 64J ★

After England's last-second drop-kick win in the 2003 Rugby World Cup, probably the most tense moment there has ever been on a rugby field for the highest number of viewers, England's Jonny Wilkinson became an unassuming hero for the nation. This had a slightly strange effect on aircraft seat allocations between London and Sydney.

The English team flew back from the World Cup on a Boeing 747-400 operated by British Airways which was renamed 'Sweet Chariot' in honour of their victory. Somehow, word got out that Wilkinson had been sitting in 64J, and for the next couple of years demand for seat 64J was significantly higher, even on standard flights.

British Airways had to issue a statement to the effect that while they would honour seat reservations for seat 64J where possible, it could not guarantee that passengers would be on the actual aircraft that had been used by the England team. Two decades later and the aircraft in question (registration G-CIVR, plane-spotting fans) is listed as withdrawn from use in April 2020. 'Withdrawn from use' is a technical term used in the aviation industry to say that that the aircraft is enjoying a well-earned retirement sitting in a field somewhere in eastern Spain. You never know, seat 64J might get stripped of its rusting carcass and find its way on to eBay at some point.

It would be interesting to know how the algorithms that manage aircraft seat demand these days would have coped with the simultaneously predictable and irrational behaviour of humans simply wanting to sit on the same seat as Wilkinson for 21 hours and eight minutes. Presumably by automatically raising the cost.

> One theme from the 2003 World Cup win that remains is Woodward's philosophy that "Winning the Rugby World Cup was not about doing one thing better, but about doing 100 things 1 per cent better." He may not have invented the term 'marginal gains' but he was a very early adopter of the theory.

• A LITTLE BOOK OF RUGBY •

"I'm no hod carrier but I would be laying bricks if he [Jonah Lomu] was running at me."

Bill Mclaren always knew the perfect phrase to describe a situation and always deserves the last word.